Stepmomming Made Easy

STRATEGIES, TOOLS, AND EVERYTHING ELSE YOU NEED TO KNOW

KRISTEN SKILES

JB JOSSEY-BASS™
A Wiley Brand

Jossey-Bass, a Wiley imprint

Published by John Wiley & Sons, Inc., Hoboken, New Jersey.
Published simultaneously in Canada.

For general information on our other products and services or for technical support, please contact our Customer Care Department within the United States at (800) 762-2974, outside the United States at (317) 572-3993 or fax (317) 572-4002.

Wiley also publishes its books in a variety of electronic formats. Some content that appears in print may not be available in electronic formats. For more information about Wiley products, visit our web site at www.wiley.com.

Library of Congress Cataloging-in-Publication Data:

Names: Skiles, Kristen author
Title: Stepmomming made easy : strategies, tools, and everything else you
   need to know / Kristen Skiles.
Description: [Hoboken] : [John Wiley & Sons Inc.], [2026] | Includes
   bibliographical references and index.
Identifiers: LCCN 2025025421 | ISBN 9781394295029 hardback |
   ISBN 9781394295043 adobe pdf | ISBN 9781394295036 epub
Subjects: LCSH: Stepmothers | Stepfamilies | Families | Parenting
Classification: LCC HQ759.92 .S57 2025 | DDC 306.874/7--dc23/eng/20250616
LC record available at https://lccn.loc.gov/2025025421

Cover Image: Wiley
Cover Design: Wiley

To "my girl" Krista, who made me a stepmom. I say it often, but I truly hit the stepdaughter jackpot with you. Thank you for your patience, kindness, and friendship the last 10 years. There's no one I'd rather laugh at silly cat videos with.

To Kevin, I could not imagine a more incredible man to call my husband and our children's father. You're everything I've ever dreamed of, and so much more than I knew was possible. Here's to forever, babe.

Contents

About the Author

Kristen Skiles is a certified Stepparent Coach, podcast host, and founder of Stepmomming.com, a leading online resource for stepmoms navigating blended family life.

With a BA in Political Science and Sociology from Pepperdine University and an MBA earned in 2016, Kristen furthered her education by becoming both a Certified Life Coach and Certified Stepparent Coach in 2020. Her background growing up in a high-conflict blended family, combined with her own journey as a stepmom since 2014, gives her a rare dual perspective: both as a stepchild and a stepmom.

Kristen's coaching philosophy centers on empowering stepmoms to reclaim their peace and identity without sacrificing their relationships. Her work blends practical strategies with deep empathy for the unique emotional challenges of stepfamily dynamics.

She hosts the *Stepmomming Made Easy* podcast and has helped thousands of stepmoms through coaching, courses, and community.

Kristen lives in Texas with her husband, their sons, and her stepdaughter. When she's not writing or coaching, she loves cheering on the Green Bay Packers, celebrating all things Christmas, and spending time with the family she always dreamed about.

Stepmomming Made Easy is her debut book.

Acknowledgments

I still can't believe I had the privilege of writing this book! It wouldn't have been possible without the best support system on the planet.

First and foremost, thank you to Sam Ofman for discovering my work, reaching out, and helping make this dream a reality. You've been an incredible mentor and guide, and *Stepmomming Made Easy* would not exist without you.

To the rest of my amazing team at Jossey-Bass and Wiley—including, but not limited to, Christine O'Connor and Rajesh Venkatraman—thank you. Your guidance, patience with my many (many!) edits, and dedication to excellence helped shape this book into the invaluable resource I know it is. I'm so proud of what we created together.

Stepmomming wouldn't be what it is today without the incredible team working passionately behind the scenes. Kalie, you're more than a best friend and colleague—you're a lifeline. Brittany and Amelia, thank you for your consistent and creative work on Stepmomming's social media. The hope and help you deliver make a difference for stepmoms across the globe.

To my family and friends—thank you for your support and unconditional love. I'm beyond blessed to be surrounded by the best people.

And to my dear husband, there's no one I'd rather do life with. Thank you for your patience as I learned how to be the best stepmom I could be, your support as I began helping others do the same, and your unwavering encouragement every step of the way. You're one in a billion, babe.

Finally, to every stepmom who picked up this book—thank you. Your trust means everything. I won't stop until every stepmom knows she deserves a stepmom life she *loves*.

Foreword

I've been on my stepmomming journey for over 20 years, and I really wish I had this book before I started. With this book, *Stepmomming*, future stepmoms can be prepared to face the practice of stepmomming with more grace and less awkwardness than I did.

As the world progresses, the definition of "family" is becoming more inclusive. It's time for some frank conversations about how to make these complicated relationships healing and nurturing for everyone involved. *Stepmomming Made Easy* is the realest, most helpful talk you'll find about the nitty-gritty of making a life that includes your partner's kids. It helps most because it's not about your partner or the kids–It's about you. It's about the things you can control, the specific support you can ask for, and the everyday solutions that will make you the best stepmom you can be.

Kristen's message is powerful: To be the best stepmom I can, I must first care for myself (in her words, "protect my peace") and the relationship that made me a stepmom. I was grateful for Kristen's reminder that I chose to be a stepmom because of my love for a person who happened to be a father. That love and that partner expanded my understanding of who I was and provided me an opportunity to be a more complete version of myself–a version I couldn't have imagined before he brought it out in me.

However, everyone knows stepmomming isn't all sunshine, and Kristen doesn't shy away from the difficulties. *Stepmomming Made Easy* is the first place that I've heard anyone acknowledge what stepmoms sacrifice. I've been very fortunate as a stepmom, but the fact remains that when I chose my partner and his kids, I demolished many potential futures I might have had. Options for my home, my education, and my work all shrunk to the geographical location of my stepkids until they finished high school. I was the only student in my doctoral school who was attending kids' school plays and concerts. Vacations were dictated by the kids' availability. Their existence defined how my husband and I spent every resource, from money to free time. My whole life plan was rewritten. No matter how enriching stepmomming can be, these sacrifices are real and deserve to be acknowledged and honored. In addition, stepmoms deserve the time to mourn and heal from their loss.

Kristen drills down on the very specific things that cause stepmoms stress, like having responsibility without having authority, perfectionistic ideals about being able to "do it all" without needing any help and being judged (sometimes even by our stepkids) in terms of amplified misogynist tropes (for women who aren't fulfilling the still-pervasive ideal of biological motherhood).

She is also very specific in offering tools that can be applied not just to stepmomming but to every other challenge of being a feminine person in the world–the unceasing demands, the impossible standards, the marginalization, and risk of isolation. Those tools include communicating your needs to your partner, protecting your core values, and finding community with other stepmoms. She reminds us we have permission to step away, to maintain boundaries, and to divest from responsibility when we need to, because our joy matters.

I hope potential stepmoms who are considering commitment to a partner with kids will read this book and speak with their partner about how they can collaborate to ensure they have access to these tools. And if a partner isn't enthusiastic about helping you be the best stepmom you can be, what does it tell you about their enthusiasm about having you in their life?

A blended family is created from loss. Divorce is one of the most difficult challenges anyone can face in their life, and divorced parents and their kids are inevitably scarred. But a wound is the place where light enters you, as Rumi, thirteenth-century poet, tells us. A stepmom can be a source of light for her partner and kids, but only so long as she has light to offer. *Stepmomming Made Easy* will teach you how to maintain your light, with guidance that is practical, positive, and realistically attainable.

A therapist once told me the love of a stepmom is different from the love of a biological mom. Maybe it is, or maybe what's different is the cultural space our love is permitted to fill.

I know this for sure: When my stepson, an actor, was in a play where his character screamed in pain, I felt a mama bear's love inside me. She took over my body–I had to grip my theater seat to keep myself from climbing over the audience to throw the boy over my shoulder and spirit him away to safety. That moment revealed to me the light I carried inside me–a fire of love as fierce as a lightning strike, as transformative as a forge. It is fueled not by sacrifice, but by my own fulfillment and boundaries and the support of my partner. With tools like those offered in *Stepmomming Made Easy*, I can shine that light into the lives of my family as stepmom, then step-grandmom, and step-great-grandmom.

So can you.

Amelia Nagoski, DMA, *New York Times* best-selling co-author of
Burnout: The Secret to Unlocking the Stress Cycle

Introduction

Hello, sweet stepmom. I'm so glad you're here. I feel like we're instant besties, don't you? We're bonded together forever by our stepmom experience.

No one else gets it like another stepmom.

This book is your safe space. You're received here with no judgment. I can practically guarantee you haven't experienced or felt something that I haven't personally gone through or that I haven't heard before from one of the thousands of stepmoms with whom I've worked. You are welcome here, without shame.

I'm Kristen, and blended family life is all I've ever really known. When I was born, my mom was in her second marriage, and I had a half sister from her first, of whom she shared custody. My parents divorced when I was two-and-a-half years old, and after living through a few of their remarriages to other people, I've lived to tell the tale.

A horrific experience dating a single dad soon out of college had me swearing off dating anyone with kids. Child in their profile pic? Swipe left! Sure, it could have been a nephew, but it's best not to tempt fate.

That is, until I found Kevin. It's almost infuriating how absolutely perfect he was. Handsome, a veteran, wicked smart, the kindest heart, ambitious, and successful … and a really incredible dad. He was the man whom I'd been searching for and had lost hope that existed. I decided he was worth bending the rules for.

We went on our first date, and it was the best first date that anyone has ever had in the history of dating, I'm sure of it. We talked for hours, practically closing down the restaurant and then walking to a nearby Best Buy to keep talking because we didn't want the magic to end. We talked about our deepest fears, our greatest dreams, and of course, his first marriage and his four-year-old daughter, Krista. (Yes, I'm Kristen Leigh, and she's Krista Lynn. … I can't make this stuff up.)

As luck would have it, he left two days later for a 15-day solo trip exploring Thailand. We stayed in touch on Facebook while he was away and had our second (just as magical) date when he returned home. We've been together ever since.

In the beginning, when we were entrenched in our own little love bubble, things were incredible. We were so good for each other, and so good together. Meeting Krista went perfectly. But as our relationship grew and I settled into the stepmom role, things became more realistic and immeasurably harder.

I've learned approximately 1,000 lessons the hard way since I met Kevin in 2014. The more I struggled, the more I sought out resources, community, and hope that a light existed at the end of the tunnel. In 2017, I started building the resources and community that were missing and that I needed in my early stepmom days. In 2018, Stepmomming was born. What began as a blog full of my stories and lessons learned as a stepmom expanded to include a support group, podcast, and tangible tools like courses and live workshops. I became a certified life coach, and then more specifically, a certified stepparent coach in 2020, and have since worked with hundreds of stepmoms personally to help each of them create a blended family life they love.

This book is the guide I needed in the thick of my stepmom struggles. It contains stories from my journey as well as those of my coaching clients. (Please note that all client names have been changed, but their stories are real.) *Stepmomming Made Easy* exists to normalize, validate, and educate.

One thing I will never tell you is to "suck it up." Your experiences and reactions are real and valid. You are not the only stepmom who is struggling or who has felt this way. Your feelings exist for a reason–your needs are not being met. Stepmomming can feel so isolating. My hope is to put words to some of the feelings and experiences with which you've struggled. Instead of suggesting you "suck it up," you'll find practical strategies and tools to build a stepmom life you love in these pages.

Not everything will be applicable to your life (at least right now), but don't let that discount the rest of this book. My goal is to write a book that helps every stepmom reclaim her peace and have a happy, fulfilling relationship and family. So, take what applies to you and leave the rest, but keep reading. It'll be worth it, I promise.

I'm really happy you're here. Welcome home, my friend.

CHAPTER 1

Perspectives

Before we dive into the practical tools that will mold your stepmomming skill set, let's start by understanding the key players in your family dynamic. Understanding how everyone else is experiencing your stepfamily will enable you to empathize with their situations and reach resolutions quicker and easier.

It's so easy to become overwhelmed by the stepmom experience and lose sight of the reality that this situation is overwhelming in other ways for everyone else too.

- ◆ Your partner is attempting to balance your needs with the demands of their ex-partner and their children.
- ◆ Your stepchild is learning how to adapt to a new parental figure in their life, a new person in their home, and (likely) new norms and rules in their home.
- ◆ Your stepchild's other parent has been jolted by the reality that another person is going to influence and be intimately involved in raising their children–a massive reality check for which they likely weren't ready.

You have every right to be overwhelmed by the stepmom experience and all that comes with this role. Your feelings and reactions are completely normal, friend. I don't want you to stay stuck in the suck, however. I want you to be able to sort through your overwhelming feelings and learn how to navigate whatever stepfamily life may throw at you.

A big part of learning how to do that is gaining an understanding of others' points of view. Not everything in stepmom life is personal–even when it feels really personal. It took me a long time to recognize that even though I was the impetus for the change (my partner met me, fell in love, and wanted to bring me into the fold), I was not responsible for the change. If it wasn't me, Kevin would have found someone else to marry (rude!), and his ex and daughter would have reacted the same way as they did when he met me.

Let's spend the next few pages going through the perspectives of each main character in this dynamic: your partner, your partner's co-parent, your stepchild(ren), and of course, you–the stepmom.

Your Partner's Perspective

For many stepmoms, the blended family experience is so overwhelming that it can be impossible to empathize with anyone else's perspective. But to be a good partner and have a successful, sustainable relationship, you must understand your partner's point of view. In this section, I provide some of the most common experiences of a stepmom's partner, and at the end, I speak specifically to the male experience. If that's not applicable to your partner, you can skip right over it and continue on to the next chapter. If your partner is male, I highly recommend that you do not skip it.

YOUR PARTNER OPERATES OUT OF FEAR

To share custody is to always live with a little bit of fear. Fear that your child will choose to stop having a relationship with you. Fear that you'll be replaced by a stepparent. Fear that your co-parent will steal them away from you. Fear that you have ruined your child's life.

This fear is an unwelcome but powerful motivator. So, the next time that your partner doesn't want to enforce the chores you two agreed upon for the kids, consider how fear might be driving that hesitancy. Or, if your partner is slow to text their child's other parent about something they disagree with, consider how a fear of retaliation might be at play.

I recently had a client lament that her partner signed his kids up for rec volleyball without discussing it with her first. She expressed frustration to me, explaining that with her three children and his two children already enrolled in other extracurricular activities, she had no idea how they'd logistically get his kids to a second activity as well. They had agreed that each child would participate in one activity at a time, but he signed them up anyway. When she asked him about his motivation, he simply said, "I can't let volleyball be the reason I lose my girls." His ex had made enough comments about the sport and threatened taking away custody so frequently that he became ruled by his fear of losing them.

YOUR PARTNER FEELS A LOT OF GUILT

Even though you and I can clearly see that sharing custody and living in two separate homes was best for your stepchild than staying in an unhappy home with unhappy parents, your partner feels like they have failed their child(ren). Society teaches them that the ideal is a nuclear family. And when that doesn't work out, they internalize it as a personal failure. Your partner is coping with their perceived failure on top of feeling like they have chosen their happiness over their child's. They wonder if they should have stuck with it for the kids. They fear that their "selfishness" (as they would describe it) has negatively affected their children and thus, feel guilty.

These guilty feelings can appear in many ways, and you likely don't need any examples (though I'll give them to you anyway). When your partner lets your stepdaughter have ice cream for dinner because she "didn't like" what you prepared, your partner's guilty parenting won out. When your partner lets your stepson stay up late playing video games, it's likely there was some guilt behind their "yes."

Disneyland Parent

If your partner is seemingly paralyzed by their guilt, it can lead them to become what's often called a *Disneyland Parent*.

A Disneyland Parent is a noncustodial parent who focuses more on enjoying time with their children and less on structure, rules, and responsibilities.

A Disneyland Parent may spoil with gifts, time, and extravagant experiences (like a trip to their namesake's Disneyland), and they will often leave most of the less-fun parenting and discipline to the custodial parent. When a single parent has restricted access to their children, they often don't want to spend it enforcing rules and aiding with homework. They'd rather spend their time doing fun activities and soaking in all of the joy.

When you're not with your children for an extended period of time, there's less of an immediate need for structure and discipline. For example, if most of the time your children are with you, it's not a school night, then there's less cause for a strict bedtime. Understandably, stepmoms partnered with Disneyland Parents become frustrated by the lack of structure and concerned about the message this parenting style sends to their stepchildren.

YOUR PARTNER WANTS YOU TO FEEL PROTECTED AND RESPECTED

Above all else, your partner wants you to feel protected and respected. They might sometimes have competing motivations (like fear), which means they fail to protect or respect you. But that doesn't change the reality that as a guiding principle, your protection and feeling respected are paramount to them. As your partner, they want those things for you.

When your partner agrees to a custody swap without communicating with you, they've acted out of impulse and desire to see their child, not intending to disrespect you in the process. When their ex disrespects you and your partner chooses not to defend you, you feel unprotected. Your partner's fears caused them not to pick that battle with their child's other parent but left you needing protection in another way.

YOUR PARTNER FEELS CAUGHT IN THE MIDDLE

Many partners feel caught in the middle of everyone else's competing desires and can't make everyone happy. The other parent wants to be your partner's teammate in raising their child together. You, understandably, want to be your partner's teammate in life, instead of their ex. And your partner's child has demands and desires of their parent too. Even worse, sometimes these three needs are all in competition with one another, and your partner knows no matter which decision they make, they're going to let someone down.

They want to keep their ex happy, so they don't lose their children. (Remember: They're ruled by fear.) They want to keep their children happy, so the children don't choose not to have a relationship with them anymore (because they're fearful). Finally, they want to keep you–their new partner–happy (because they want you to feel protected and respected). Do you see how decisions that seem easy to you and I aren't as straightforward to our partners?

In coaching sessions with stepmoms and their partners, I often hear the partner express, "I just can't make anyone happy! I'm failing everyone!" This isn't uncommon. Our partners are exasperated trying to navigate the dynamics in a way that maintains harmony.

YOUR PARTNER NEEDS TO KNOW YOU BELIEVE IN THEM

We've already explored the ego hit that sharing custody of their child and not having the praised nuclear family was to your partner. They're a bit vulnerable, heading into a new relationship, so treat them with care. Make sure your partner knows you believe in them, you trust them to protect you, and you know they make good decisions. This confidence builds them up individually and within your relationship.

You might be thinking, "Kristen, of course, I believe in them! I wouldn't be wasting my time with them if I didn't!" and I hear you loud and clear! But are your actions communicating that? For example, if you're reviewing all your partner's texts to the other parent before they send them, you might be communicating to your partner that you don't trust them to communicate effectively without your oversight.

Our partners were capable adults before we came into the picture. They need to know that we realize that, and we trust them to provide for and protect us.

YOUR PARTNER NEEDS TO TRUST THAT THEIR EX IS A GOOD PERSON

If you're eager to bad-mouth the ex and your partner seems hesitant to join in the bashing, it's likely because your partner needs to trust that their ex is a good person. Think about it this way: Your partner is relying on the other parent to keep their children alive and healthy at least part of the time. They're not going to want to focus on that person's faults and every way that person might negatively impact their children.

Men Are Naturally Wired to Be Protectors and Providers

If you are coupled with a man, it's important to recognize that men naturally want to provide for and protect the ones they love. Further, a man will always protect before he can provide. (This stems back to the earliest days of humanity, where if a man didn't protect, there might not be anyone to provide for.) So, if your partner feels that his child is being threatened or hurt in a situation, he will protect his child before he can provide support to you.

One final reminder: Your partner is learning as they go too. As stepmoms, we might expect our partner to have it all figured out, because they're bringing us into a complex dynamic. But the reality is, they're learning how to navigate this situation also. A little empathy and grace can go a very long way.

The Other Parent's Perspective

One of the most villainized people in stepmom circles is their partner's ex–their stepchild's other parent. And it's often for good reason! But the better you understand the other parent's perspective, the less frustrating and infuriating their actions will become. You'll understand their motivations (even if you don't agree with them), and you'll be able to shake it off easier.

I want to preface this description of the other parent's perspective with a couple of reminders:

◆ Not every single thing mentioned in this chapter will apply to your co-parent. That's totally normal!
◆ Approach this chapter with an open mind. Be willing to learn and reflect upon, without defensiveness, what might be motivating your stepchild's other parent. This book is a resource to help you grow and learn.

YOUR STEPCHILD'S OTHER PARENT DIDN'T PLAN TO CO-PARENT

Yes, even if they are the ones who initiated the breakup (or if they were never together to begin with), you were never part of their thought process. The other parent simply knew that living in one home as a family, alongside your now-partner, wasn't a viable option and opted for two homes and shared child custody.

When you entered the picture, they were forced to accept the reality that a new person might be parenting their child and everything that comes with that fact. This includes someone else's values, parenting styles, influence over their children, and that their child might enjoy spending time with that other person.

I respect that you might believe the other parent should've known to expect their ex to recouple at some point. I also believed this. However, we were a nonissue, until we weren't.

YOUR STEPCHILD'S OTHER PARENT DOESN'T KNOW OR CHOOSE YOU

You know you're a good person, and your partner obviously believes that too. Yet, the other parent is predisposed to not trust you. You're a stranger, and they want to protect their child. The other parent often needs more than their ex's endorsement of a new partner to fully trust and embrace a new co-parent.

The other parent didn't choose to have you in their life, and they likely don't want to be a co-parent with you. They do know your partner. They agreed to co-parent their child together.

THE OTHER PARENT EXPECTS YOU TO STAY IN THE SHADOWS

A new stepmom expects that the status quo will change now that she has entered the picture, and that she will be brought into the co-parenting fold. Yet, that's virtually the opposite of how the other parent views your role. They expect nothing to change, and they plan to continue co-parenting with your partner, without interference or opinion from anyone else.

Is it shortsighted and naive to think that someone wouldn't factor their new partner into decisions? Yes. But it's the reality of co-parenting. Co-parents want to cling to the old family unit for the sake of simplicity and maintaining control. They want that old family unit to be compartmentalized, unrelated to and unaffected by anything else. They think their ex-partner's private life and personal decisions (including a new relationship) shouldn't affect that protected bubble.

THE OTHER PARENT BELIEVES YOU SHOULD KNOW "YOUR PLACE"

Because the other parent believes the stepmom is a nonissue and shouldn't affect the co-parenting relationship with their co-parent, they believe the stepmom should keep her opinions to herself. According to the other parent, just because a stepmom is dating someone with kids doesn't mean she should have a say in the children's lives–that is the responsibility for the two original parents.

It's why you might hear things like "Know your place" or "Stay in your lane." The other parent firmly believes you don't have a place in co-parenting alongside your partner or parenting their children. (Yes, even if their new partner does co-parent and/or parent. Aren't hypocrisy and the stepmom double standard fun?)

NEITHER OF YOU LIKES ANOTHER PERSON HAVING A SAY

I know that another person–especially your partner's ex–having a say in your life is excruciating for you. It's painful for them as well. Not only do they not get to choose who will be in their child's life, now the impact of that choice is being felt within their home. Believe it or not, you also get a say in your stepchild's other parent's life too.

The way that you encourage your partner and the little seeds that you plant with them about how to parent and co-parent, are felt dramatically by the other parent. Every shift in your partner–no matter how tiny or how positive–feels seismic to their co-parent. But your impact isn't only indirect; the role modeling and influencing you have on your stepchildren directly also has a sizable impact on their other parent.

I include a silly example, but poignant one, nonetheless. Growing up, my mom made us Kraft macaroni and cheese. But my stepmom served up Velveeta shells and cheese, and I swear to you it changed my life. I arrived home raving about my stepmom's delicious macaroni and how I never wanted Kraft macaroni again. I wanted Velveeta only. My mom, understandably, was frustrated that my stepmom's choice now meant my mom would need to buy two to three times more expensive macaroni and cheese or face my disappointment.

(And possibly hear a diatribe about how my stepmom's cooking was so much better–ouch!)

From the smaller influences like the macaroni and cheese you buy and the way you encouraged your stepdaughter to try out for volleyball, to the bigger impact you can have on your stepchildren, like the religion you practice and the support you provide your partner in their pursuit for additional custody, you do have a say in the other parent's life too. And it's possibly a very disruptive say.

YOU IMPAIR THE OTHER PARENT'S CONTROL

As a stepmom, you have the power to take control away from the other parent, even if subconsciously. If your partner invites you to a parent-teacher conference or a little league game, the other parent doesn't have as much control over the setting as they did before.

When you move in with your partner and their children–or even take a vacation together–the other parent might feel completely powerless. In this type of immersive environment where you have a major influence on the children, the other parent has virtually no control over any of it.

It's an important lesson for the other parent to learn, but it's hard to lose control, especially when your children are involved.

Changing Dynamics When a Stepmom Enters the Scene

Many stepmoms bolster the confidence of their partners so much that they begin advocating for themselves and their relationship with their children more.

Before the stepmom came into the picture, her partner might have been more cooperative and less opinionated. Sometimes, a dynamic of "You make the decisions, and I'll go along with them," is the easiest option. It's the path of least resistance–no risk of rocking the boat with the other parent, mitigated risk of losing their child, and less decisions to be made–everyone just goes with the flow. It works well when the parent is single.

But after a repartnering, the stepmom understandably doesn't want the other parent making so many decisions for her. She also sees the value her partner has as a parent and encourages them to live up to their parenting potential. As a result, the stepmom's partner begins to push back on their co-parent for more custody time, equal decision-making power, and a healthier, more cooperative dynamic. The other parent is obviously annoyed. Things were working just fine with the "co-parenting means I make decisions, and you agree to them" dynamic before the stepmom entered the picture. You've disrupted the other parent's life. This frustration is compounded by their belief that you should know your place and stay in the background.

Is the stepmom wrong for encouraging her partner and bolstering their confidence? Of course not! Is the parent wrong for wanting to be more involved in their child's life? Of course not! Is the other parent wrong for being annoyed that their ex repartnered and now everything is evolving? It's a natural reaction in my opinion. Must things shift to accommodate a new partner and those changing dynamics? Yes. But those growing pains are natural, and the ex is entitled to their feelings (even if their original dynamic wasn't sustainable or equal).

THE OTHER PARENT BELIEVES YOU SHOULD KNOW AND HONOR ALL THEIR BOUNDARIES

Your stepchild's other parent has a mental list of things that aren't okay for the stepmom to do. Oftentimes, this list isn't communicated, and the stepmom has no idea that she's crossing a boundary. It's possible that the other parent doesn't even realize it's a boundary until it's been crossed.

The other parent perceives their boundaries and needs as more important than yours as a stepmom, and they expect you to play according to their rules. I'll discuss later why this isn't practical, but for now, I want you to recognize the other parent's viewpoint and how their beliefs are affecting their actions. The goal of this chapter is to understand their perspective, even when you disagree with it.

Some common boundaries the other parent might prefer that a stepmom not cross are taking their daughter to get a haircut, attending parent-teacher conferences, and being on their child's sports team app.

They might perceive these things as reserved for the "real" parents. (I could go on a tirade about how offensive the "real" clarifier is, but I'll save that soapbox for another day and just say this: You are as real as it gets, my friend. Your sacrifices, effort, and love are so very real.)

YOU ACT AS A MIRROR TO THE OTHER PARENT'S INSECURITIES AND PERCEIVED FLAWS

As a stepmom, you're in the unique position to be a source of comparison for the other parent (because they worry their children will be comparing the two of you). No parent wants to be seen as anything but a superhero in the eyes of their children, so the idea of someone "better" coming into their lives feels threatening.

Maybe you have your master's or doctorate degree, and they wish they'd attended college. Maybe you're an incredible chef, and they're like me and can prepare a mean bowl of cereal. Perhaps you're a literal supermodel, and the other parent feels insecure about their appearance.

No matter the issue, you figuratively hold up a mirror to the other parent's insecurities and perceived flaws.[1] And they might disapprove of you for it.

THE OTHER PARENT DISLIKES WHAT YOU REPRESENT

It's entirely possible that if the other parent doesn't like you or pushes you away, it's not personal. They don't dislike you; they simply dislike what you represent. You are living, breathing proof of the failure of their relationship, the demise of their family, and the guilt and fear that they've given their child a "broken" family and childhood.

Perhaps you're the individual who their ex finally improved and stepped up for in ways that the other parent wanted for so many years. In some ways, you might be seen as living the life that the other parent dreamed of, and they feel as if they weren't good enough for it, but you are. When this happens, the experience feels deeply personal.

THE OTHER PARENT FEARS THEIR KIDS WILL LOVE YOU MORE

A final extremely personal reality is that the ex might fear losing their children to you. You're seen as the fun new parent, and they might fear that their children will love you more. It's an illogical fear, as children always need their original parents, craving their attention, approval, and love. It's all but impossible to replace those needs. And yet, it's a powerful and very real fear to experience.

My hope is that all this information has given you a clearer depiction of the parent on the other side of your co-parenting dynamic. Who they are, what they desire, and what they fear. This knowledge might feel overwhelming at first, but in time you'll be able to use it to better understand their actions. And once you can recognize their motivation for what it is, instead of the personal attack that it feels like, you'll have more freedom to show up unapologetically in your blended family.

Your Stepchild's Perspective

Stepchildren might just be the least considered group in this entire blended family dynamic. Children are tough, and sometimes we take that for granted. As a child of divorce and subsequently, a stepchild, myself, I have a huge heart for all the children tied up in these complicated dynamics. They're resilient and adaptable without question, but they're also dealing with a lot going on just below the surface.

Once you learn more about your stepchild's perspective, you'll better understand why they act and react in the ways they do. You'll then become a better guide and support to them as a result.

THEY FEAR THAT THEY'LL BE REPLACED

My biggest fear when my dad remarried was that I would lose him to his new partner. I worried that he'd met someone who would monopolize his time, and that he didn't need me anymore. This fear was amplified when, after marrying my second stepmom, he accepted his dream job and moved across the country. My stepmom didn't cause that, of course, but it felt personal to my 8-year-old heart.

It's natural when you start dating someone new, that they receive much of your time and attention. The relationship is new and exciting, and you want to spend all your available time with said person. It's also likely your stepchild has sensed your partner's draw to you, and the subsequent (subconscious, unintentional, and likely subtle) withdrawal from them. This withdrawal is an actualization of their fear that they are being replaced by their new stepparent. So, if your stepchild seems extra clingy to your partner or avoidant of you, they might be ruled by this fear right now.

I sometimes have clients tell me their stepchild has decided to stop coming to their home during their custodial time. Oftentimes, I'm also told that the child doesn't reach out to the stepmom's partner (the child's parent) to maintain a relationship. As the daughter whose dad moved across the country and realizing my fear that I wasn't the most important thing in his world, I resonate with these kids and their feelings deeply. They want their parent to make the effort–to show them they're important, irreplaceable, and, above all, loved.

THEY'RE GRIEVING THE LOSS OF THEIR FAMILY UNIT

Of course, your stepchild wants their parents together, because it feels like a major loss to them! Don't we all crave peace, love, and normalcy? Kids don't have the same context that we do as adults. They don't understand infidelity, falling out of love, and irreconcilable differences the same way you and I do. They just know things would be simpler if their parents were together and in love. They crave the fairy-tale family.

When we enter the picture as their stepmom, that loss becomes more evident, more permanent. We symbolize that loss to them, which is why we're sometimes the target of their emotional outbursts and attacks. They must mourn that loss and cope with emotions that are likely to feel too big for their little bodies. In fact, research shows the recoupling of a parent is harder on children than the original separation.[2]

LIFE WITH TWO HOMES IS TOUGH

Our stepchildren flit between two homes with two different layouts, different house rules, and different parenting styles, just to start. Expecting them to do it flawlessly is impractical, unrealistic, and insensitive.

When my dad moved away and I only spent summers and school holidays with him, it took me a long time to feel "at home" there. I distinctly remember the time my stepmom gave me permission to go into the pantry to get snacks if I wanted them between meals. She stated it like it should have been obvious, but I needed that permission because I felt like a visitor, even though it was my dad's home and I was a member of the family.

Navigating between two homes and adjusting to the culture of each home is a lot to manage. Add in the extra responsibility of bringing necessary belongings between homes, and the challenge compounds. Be patient with your stepchildren when they forget your expectations, or when they act out because the transition is challenging. Encourage your partner to give them extra attention and reminders to make transitions easier.

THEY LONG FOR CONTROL

As children with separated parents, a custody schedule, and two homes, our stepchildren are longing for control. So much of life has happened *to* them, and they simply want control over some of it. They didn't get to choose for their parents not to be together, or choose to have two homes, or choose their new stepmom. We all want to be autonomous beings who live a life we want, not one dictated by others' actions.

You represent a long history of decisions being thrust upon them, and it's natural if they begin to fight back. They have control over their actions and reactions. So, when they begin to fight back, they are controlling what they can. To help them feel more comfortable with the changes and more in control, present them with choices wherever you can. Ask your stepdaughter if she wants to go to the library or the bookstore. Ask your stepson which video game he wants to play today. Let your stepchild choose the vegetable you prepare with dinner. Allow them to choose their outfits each morning.

They are craving control, so you must help them to find it in healthy ways.

THEY DON'T AUTOMATICALLY RESPECT STEPPARENTS

As their parent's chosen partner, you don't automatically gain your stepchild's respect.[3] You must earn their trust, and subsequently, their respect. If you grew up in a home like the one I grew up in, you probably think that being an adult makes you worthy of their respect. And while I agree that, yes, your stepchildren should say hello to you when they walk into a room that you're in and that they should not disrespect you, your respect as a parental figure must be earned.

I'll delve into much more about this in Chapter 5, but for now, it's important to recognize that your stepchildren aren't seeking another disciplinarian, and that they'll have a very difficult time respecting your attempts to discipline them if they don't respect you. Focus first on building a relationship with them, before stepping into a parental role.

YOU'LL NEVER BE SEEN THE SAME AS THEIR PARENTS

It's a bit early in the book for me to be dropping this bomb on you, but we're going there, even if only briefly. Your stepchildren see a difference between you and their original parents, and they always will. This absolutely does not mean you can't have a beautiful, meaningful relationship. It also doesn't have to mean they wouldn't be devastated if something happened to you. But it is a different relationship.

One of the very tangible ways you will see this in daily life is that children forgive their original parents much easier than they forgive their stepparents.[3] Let your partner be the one to deliver the punishment. Avoid being the disciplinarian when you can. You're the scapegoat, and it's unfair, but it's reality.

Recognize that your relationship with them is conditional. It's conditional on you loving their parent and being in a relationship with that parent. What if something happens and you separate, like their original parents did? It's natural if your stepchildren are hesitant to go all-in on you.

And then, of course, there's the natural desire in many of us to please our original parents. We crave their love, admiration, respect, and attention. Your stepchild receiving those things from you is valuable, but it's not quite the same. It can't replace receiving those things from their original parent.

I've worked with several full-time stepmoms whose co-parents decided they didn't want to be very involved in their children's lives. These stepmoms all shared similar experiences: navigating conversations with their stepchildren who idolize their absentee parent. The stepmom must bite her tongue when their stepchild shares an opinion of or experience with their other parent that varies dramatically from the stepmom's opinion of and experience with them. Children need to believe their parents are good role models and love them.

NORMS AND HABITS EXISTED BEFORE YOU ENTERED THE HOME

Your partner and their child had a certain way of doing things before you entered the home. They might have dropped their towels on the bathroom floor after bath time, gone to bed too late, or chosen not to eat as many fruits and vegetables as health professionals recommend.

I know you know better. I know you can fix these things. I know that it probably irritates the living daylights out of you. But recognize that you cannot change everything at once. It is extremely important that you honor existing norms and habits when you move in together as a family. You can save the towels from mildew, recommend a reasonable bedtime, and introduce more produce in due time. But if you try to change everything at once, it will create a culture shock for the child, and they'll blame you for ruining everything. Admittedly, it's a slight dramatization, but probably not by much.

You'd feel uprooted and uneasy if one day your partner invited your mother-in-law to live with you, and she told you that you were doing many things wrong, and that you needed to fix them all at once, right? You'd probably want to chuck a zucchini across the kitchen at her or tell her she smells like a mildewy towel, instead of recognizing the good intentions behind her recommendations. It's the same for our stepchildren.

Your Perspective as the Stepmom

After exploring everyone else's perspectives in this dynamic, it's finally time to pen the tale of the stepmom. I saved this perspective for last so that you'd be the most open to the others and to validate your own perspective. If you take nothing else away from this book, I hope you know that you are not alone. Your struggles, your reactions, and your feelings: They're all so normal. You are not struggling because you aren't cut out to be a stepmom; you are struggling because this role is hard.

A STEPMOM VIEWS HER STEPCHILD THROUGH A LENS OF RESPONSIBILITY

An original parent will love their children. Yet not every stepmom will love her stepchildren, at least not in the way she expected to love them, or the way she loves her own children. A romantic love for your partner does not automatically translate to a parental love for a stepchild. Even stepmoms like me, who love their stepchildren, still see them primarily through a lens of responsibility. We think about ensuring their needs are met and that our stepchildren are being cared for in a way that prepares them to be happy, productive, successful adults.

When a stepmom hears that her stepchildren are unexpectedly going to be staying over an extra night that week, one of her first thoughts will be, "Did I plan enough for dinner that night?" or "Is the house clean enough?" There will likely be responsibility tied to her response in some fashion. But our partners? They're just stoked for more time with their children! Their response will be primarily–if not entirely–from a place of love.

STEPMOMS ARE DIFFERENT WHEN THEIR STEPCHILDREN ARE HOME

Directly related to our response of responsibility is the fact that as stepmoms, we're different when our stepchildren are in our home. Our partners are the same when their children are in our home or their other home, but stepmoms are not. We're on alert. There are little adjustments, like listening for signs our stepchildren need us and making sure they're fed and being cared for. Then there are the bigger adjustments, like feeling on guard and wanting to be on our best behavior. For some, it can even feel like our stepchildren are carrying around video cameras, reporting our actions back to their other parent.

Think about it this way: When your stepson is home, you always wear a bra. When he's not, you probably rip that thing off when you're halfway through the door after a long day at work. When your stepdaughter is at her other home, you can breastfeed your baby whenever and wherever you need to, but when she's home, you opt for more private spaces or to wear a cover when in her presence. We are different–arguably less comfortable–when our stepchildren are home. It's a stark contrast to our partner's experience, whose heart is full because their whole family is home.

A STEPMOM OFTEN FEELS SHE'S DAMNED IF SHE DOES, AND DAMNED IF SHE DOESN'T

When it comes to a stepmom's relationship with her stepchild, everyone has an opinion. If she steps up and is really engaged and involved in her stepchild's life, the ex will complain she has over-stepped. If she takes more of a support role, society will be quick to pounce: "Her stepchildren deserve better! Why doesn't she treat them the way she treats her own children? Why is her partner with someone who doesn't love her stepchildren enough?!"

It's exhausting and unfair, which leads me to my next point.

A STEPMOM OFTEN FEELS UNDER APPRECIATED AT BEST AND UNAPPRECIATED AT WORST

Stepmomming can feel so sacrificial. Many of you gave up pieces of yourselves for your relationship, and it's common to feel resentful when your effort isn't acknowledged. Here are just a few examples of big and small things that have contributed to feeling underappreciated in my own stepmom life:

- I left the house I bought and decorated as my own, to move 30 minutes away into a new community with my new husband and his daughter. I left behind my sister's family I was extremely close with, my tutoring clients, and the community I called home. There was no real discussion of where we'd live; Krista's school was near Kevin's home, so it was assumed I would move for our relationship. I know Kevin appreciates me, but I'm not sure he recognizes how big a sacrifice I made.

- My stepdaughter requested I buy cucumbers, lime juice, and TAJÍN to pack in her lunch. At the grocery store, I was thrilled to find TAJÍN with lime! SCORE! I knew she'd be thrilled. Until … she wasn't. "No, I really need lime juice. This isn't the same," she told me. That bottle of TAJÍN with lime still mocks me every time I go into the pantry.

- I love birthdays. Everything about them makes me giddy. The idea that one day gets to be all about you–it's magical. I've worked hard to make all my stepdaughter's birthdays as special as possible since the day I met her. I remember the year we took her to go indoor skydiving and to hibachi (her choice) for dinner on her big day. There was the birthday party that I (her stepmom) arranged at a local aquatic center, so she could have a swim party in March. There was also her 13th birthday theme of "Krista's favorite things," where her mom and I collaborated on the menu to ensure all her favorite foods would be there. But I was the one who went a step farther and surprised her with a silent disco. I can honestly say I have given my all to every single one of Krista's birthdays.

Fast-forward to last year. I threw a massive "Grahammy's" party for my biological son, Graham's, first birthday. It was admittedly extravagant and unnecessary. We struggled for years to get pregnant, and I went all in on the red-carpet theme. Throughout the party prep and during the actual party, I was told three separate times by my in-laws to be sure that I put the same budget and effort into Krista's 16th birthday party (which was a year and a half in the future, I might add). By scrutinizing my actions for my son, their comments immediately made me feel like all the effort I had consistently put into celebrating Krista's birthdays for nine years were not seen or appreciated.

THERE'S A DOUBLE STANDARD FOR STEPMOMS

As my birthday party example illustrates, there's a massive double standard for stepmoms. We are held to a much higher (impossibly high, I might argue) standard than moms are. Would a mom have been reminded to be thinking about her other child's birthday in two years' time, while planning her one-year-old's birthday? Possibly, but I really doubt it. And how much support does your mom friend get in the group chat when she asks, "Is the school break over yet? These kids are driving me crazy!" However, you don't dare express the same sentiment as a stepmom, or you'll be reprimanded and reminded you should be grateful for the time you get with them. You might hear things like, "If you're that annoyed with them, let them be with their other parent who would LOVE to be with them!" Every parent gets tired during long school breaks. As a stepmom, you're entitled to the exact same feelings and responses as others. Don't listen to the double standard.

THE EVIL STEPMOM TROPE IS EXHAUSTING

The evil stepmom trope dates back to Greek mythology, but Disney breathed new life into it in the early twentieth century (Graves[4]; Snow White and the Seven Dwarfs[5]; Disney's Cinderella[6]). As a stepmom, it can feel like you're fighting against the "evil" stereotype at every turn. You must work overtime to prove you're not evil, instead of focusing your efforts on your homes and families. It might feel as if your actions are especially scrutinized, attempting to detect malicious intent. When what you really need is a bit of grace and the benefit of the doubt.

STEPMOMS ARE MOURNING THE FAMILY LIFE THEY THOUGHT THEY'D HAVE

We didn't dream of growing up to become stepmoms; in fact, not to beat a dead horse, but Disney made sure no one idolized this role. We dreamed of falling madly in love with someone, having many adventures together, and deciding together to start a family. We weren't planning to join an existing one. Because of all the ways that those dynamics have shifted and differ so dramatically from our vision and dreams, we're left grieving the loss of how life was "supposed" to look. It doesn't mean our family isn't incredible and we aren't planning for forever with our partner, but it does require a massive perspective shift.

STEPMOMS FEEL LIKE OUTSIDERS IN OUR OWN FAMILIES AND HOMES

When we became stepmoms, we knew that our partner had a past that didn't include us. We knew there was an ex, at least one child, and a corresponding history. But I think I speak for the collective group when I say that we had no idea all the ways that the past would actually show up in our daily lives and affect us. When the parent-child relationship predates the stepmom-partner relationship, stepmoms are "stuck outsiders."[7] Norms, habits, inside jokes, house rules, behavioral expectations … they all existed before we entered the family. We're left having to learn their way of life and find a way to fit in with them.

This shows up in big ways, like when our partners agree to schedule changes with our stepchild's other parent, and we're the last to know that our home will have an extra person this evening. We also feel like outsiders in small moments too. Like when our partner and their child share a couch for movie night, and we're sitting on the other side of the room. The feelings are there when they reminisce about something that happened before we entered the picture. And for stepmoms who move into their partner's home from their prior relationship, every piece of furniture or decor can remind them they're an outsider, trying to fit into someone else's family. We are outsiders, and it feels like it.

STEPMOMS OFTEN FEEL LIKE THEIR RELATIONSHIP WITH THEIR PARTNER IS ON HOLD DURING CUSTODIAL TIME

We've already explored the partner's perspective in this dynamic. We know how much they miss their children while they're at their other home, and the guilt that drives some of their decisions. It's understandable that they're eager to see their children during their custodial time and want to make them feel like a priority. However, many stepmoms feel like they lose their partner during this time.[8] It can feel as if you're swapping between two dramatically different lives: one with a loving relationship and one where you're an outsider while your partner is an attentive parent.

This is amplified for stepmoms who have children with their partners (aka "ours babies"). When your partner is focusing most of their attention on your stepchildren during their custodial time, it can feel like your children have a part-time parent now too: one who only really engages during the other child's noncustodial time.

STEPMOMS MUST DEAL WITH THEIR PARTNER'S EX FOR LIFE

Whether involved or uninvolved, dead or alive, stepmoms are dealing with their partner's ex in some capacity for the rest of their lives.[9] I don't know about you, but someone my partner chose to sleep with is not at the top of my list of people I'd choose to interact with on a regular basis in any other scenario. She also gets to make decisions that affect me, which is a whole other soapbox altogether.

And even if the other parent isn't present, their child likely still idolizes them, wants to talk about them, and craves their love. It's not something we can replace, so the other parent's impact on their child is something with which we're dealing.

I think this is especially painful for stepmoms of children from one-night stands. One night of fun for them has led to a lifetime of co-parenting and stepparenting for you.

Stepmoms Whose Stepchildren Don't Have Another Parent

Stepmomming when your stepchildren have lost their other parent is a uniquely challenging situation for a variety of reasons.

First, your stepchildren feel an intense loyalty bind to the parent they've lost, and they're often hesitant to embrace your presence in their lives, fearing it is a betrayal of that parent. The child doesn't want you (or anyone) to replace their other parent, and your presence feels like a threat to that goal.

Second, you have full custody! Stepmomming without a break is tough. As a full-time stepmom, it's especially important that you set boundaries, define a sustainable role for yourself in your family, and make time for self-care.

Third, your partner might have expectations you're unwilling or unable to meet. They might be jaded by the idea of a family made whole again or expect you to step in and fill in a role you're not interested in filling. (To reiterate, your stepchildren don't want you to fill that role either). If your partner is looking at you to fix what you didn't break, use what you learn in this book to confidently step into the role that feels right for you.

STEPMOMS DON'T UNDERSTAND WHY THE OTHER PARENT DOESN'T APPRECIATE THEM

While we're on the topic of the ex, let's dig in a bit deeper. Many stepmoms wonder, "Why is your ex so resistant to someone who cares about your children?" If a stepmom is confident that she's a good person and adds value to her stepchild's life, it can be especially frustrating when the other parent pushes her away or undermines her role in said child's life. It feels obvious that your partner wouldn't have introduced you to their kids if you weren't a good person. And yet, the other parent doesn't operate under the same assumption, so it feels like a personal attack.

STEPMOMS FEEL ALONE IN THEIR FEELINGS

As a stepmom, it can feel like no one gets what you're going through. Plus, you feel embarrassed and guilty for a lot of the experiences you have (feeling jealous of your stepchildren, feeling insecure about your partner's prior relationship, feeling like an outsider in your family, being relieved when the kids leave). When these experiences aren't normalized, it leaves stepmoms feeling isolated and even more discouraged.

I spend the rest of this book discussing strategies for overcoming these struggles and creating a stepmom life that you'll love. But the very first step is to normalize and validate, and you can do so with some quick wins, as discussed in the next chapter. You are not alone, and I'm so glad you are here.

CHAPTER 2

Quick Wins

I want to be clear that this book shouldn't be considered as the "fad diet" for stepmoms. You won't lose 1,000 pounds of blended family expectations overnight. But you will learn healthy habits and life-changing skills to create a stepmom life you love … over time. Such skills take time to learn and to perfect. But if you're anything like me, you're impatient and really want to see results NOW. You've struggled long enough, and you don't want to wait another minute.

I get it. It's why this chapter covers the "Quick Wins" that give you some relief and encouragement to continue on your journey. The next few chapters take you through some of the most impactful tools I teach my stepmom coaching clients. They're things that won't take long to implement but get big results.

We'll start by covering core values. Each of us has personal values that are core to our feeling stable and at peace. When a core value is violated, our nervous system is activated.[10] It triggers your fight-or-flight response with which you're likely very familiar. Understanding your core values helps to identify why you're triggered in your blended family, and how to restore calm.

Further, discussing your core values with your partner (and learning theirs) deepens your relationship. You'll learn to understand, respect, and protect one another on a much deeper level. Knowing your core values is one of the single best tools I've learned as a stepmom, and I'm excited to share it with you.

Next, we'll dive into house rules and family meetings. Both aren't the sexiest of topics, but they're important ones! Behavior expectations set the entire family up for success and give you all the best chance of comfort and security in your home. While family meetings sound pretty boring, they're a great vehicle for communication. I'll also provide you with some ideas to make them more fun for everyone involved. Once you have set rules in place to protect your core values from being violated, you'll feel less on guard and more at peace. You can then use that time and space to start working through the rest of what this book has to teach you.

Finally, I'll give you a few tasks to implement into your daily routine. If you can work them into your schedule, you'll begin to see a positive shift in your mindset and relationships. I know how hectic stepmom life is, and I wouldn't ask you to add anything else to your busy schedule if I didn't firmly believe it would improve your life.

I've seen the transformation these Quick Wins (and all the book's strategies, for that matter) have made in my life and the lives of countless coaching clients. I know that if you do the work, you're going to see a massive shift. Let's get started!

Protecting Your Core Values

"The most important thing in communication is hearing what isn't said."[11]

– Peter Drucker, social scientist and author

When I first became a stepmom, I felt like I was being triggered or provoked all day, every day. I was in a constant state of fight-or-flight, and it was exhausting. Numerous things, both large and small, set me off. I wanted to run, to cry, to scream. It was too much for me to handle. I'd repeatedly ask myself, "What did I sign up for?"

It wasn't until I learned about my core values that I could understand, cope with, and prevent my triggers. Core, or personal, values are the things that we hold most dear. They are those values that make us feel balanced and at peace. Each of us has many things that we value, but there are typically three to five that greatly contribute to personal harmony.

Core values are so innate to us that you might not even realize how they influence your needs and mindset. Behind every triggering event, there's a violated core value.

Values are shaped throughout our lives, and they might be influenced by:

◆ Your upbringing
◆ Life experiences
◆ Religious beliefs
◆ Regional culture
◆ Relationship history
◆ Past trauma

Let's dig into each of those a bit more.

YOUR UPBRINGING

Growing up, I must've heard "Respect your elders" every single day of my childhood. It is as engrained in me as my knowledge that the sky is blue.

So, when I became a stepmom, and my stepdaughter wasn't raised with the same authoritative parenting style as I was, I found myself very triggered in situations when I perceived her words or actions as disrespectful.

Because respect is a core value of mine due to my upbringing, I must be respected by my stepdaughter, her mom and stepdad, my partner, my in-laws, and the other players in this dynamic. When I feel disrespected, my body reacts with a fight-or-flight response.

LIFE EXPERIENCES

You had a life before you became a stepmom, and the experiences you had are responsible for shaping what you need on a daily basis. I can think of no better example of this than my dear client, Amy. Amy worked hard putting herself through college and medical school, and she had a successful career as a doctor when she met her current husband, Jeff. He and his three kids, whom he shares custody of, moved into her home when they married.

Jeff, a teacher, paid his ex-wife hundreds of dollars in child support every month. He also covered all school, health, and extracurricular expenses. Amy loved that Jeff took such good care of his children, but she felt defensive and uncomfortable whenever he suggested they send more money to his ex to pay for something more for his children.

Amy assured me it wasn't about the money as much as it felt like the principle of it all. She didn't want to feel like his ex was managing their money, or her money. Amy had a core value of financial security. So, every time Jeff's ex wanted more money or threatened to take them to court, it felt like their financial security was threatened and triggered Amy's fight-or-flight response.

RELIGIOUS BELIEFS

A few years back, I was working with a sweet client, Monica. She shared her struggles with me. "I respect that my stepdaughter already has two parents and doesn't need me to step into that role for her, but I'm still SO bothered by the fact that she lives with her boyfriend!"

Monica's stepdaughter's cohabitation (and assumed premarital sex) were contrary to Monica's religious beliefs. Whenever her stepdaughter's living arrangements or boyfriend were mentioned–especially when her husband asked if they could help pay rent for his daughter–Monica was triggered.

Her religious beliefs were critically tied to her core values, and when that core value was violated, Monica's fight-or-flight response was launched.

REGIONAL CULTURE

Amir and Fatima, a stepcouple with whom I had the pleasure of working, grew up in a culture where family is incredibly important. It's the top priority and comes before self.

Fatima, as Amir's second wife and his daughter's stepmom, wasn't held in the highest regard by his family of origin. His mom and sister were especially wary of her and judged her interactions with her stepdaughter extensively. In response, Fatima withdrew from those relationships. She needed clarity of mind to effectively show up for her stepfamily without fear of judgment by her husband's family.

Amir felt defensive and hurt when his wife started pulling away from family gatherings. Her withdrawal deeply challenged his core value of family, leaving him unsettled when they couldn't all get along and be together peacefully.

RELATIONSHIP HISTORY

A stepmom client of mine, Alicia, had been burned in her first marriage. Her husband had cheated on her for years, without her ever finding out. When she met her new husband, she valued trust over everything else.

When he broke a seemingly innocuous promise to her, it devastated her, causing her to question their entire relationship. Alicia needed to fully trust her new partner, because it had been lacking in her first marriage.

PAST TRAUMA

It's no secret that trauma shapes who we become. It leaves its mark deep inside us and transforms the values we need to feel secure. For example, a stepmom who spent her childhood in various foster homes would deeply value family and loyalty. She would benefit from a partner who's cognizant of this value need and actively works to include the stepmom in the new family dynamic. Outsider feelings would be amplified for her, reminiscent of her childhood, and triggering her family core value.

No matter what the origin of our core values are, they affect our ability to connect and communicate healthily. Until our core values are restored, we're unable to process the event productively. This restoration allows our bodies to terminate the fight-or-flight reflex and reclaim peace and balance.

Our brains have a very challenging time flipping between our emotional side and logical side. Once our core values have been violated and we've flipped over to the emotional side, all logic flies out the window. Say one of my primary core values is communication, and you've just told me that we're expected to celebrate a holiday at the ex's house without discussing it with me first. As a result, I'll be incapable of having a productive, civil, healthy conversation with you, until I've received proper communication from you.

Activity: Determine Your Core Values

I want you to take some time with the core values listed in Figure 2.1 and really reflect on and rank which ones strike a chord with you. Which values are important to you? Which ones really resonate with you?

CORE VALUES

Acceptance	Emotional awareness	Joy	Risk taking
Accomplishment	Equality	Justice	Rule following
Adventure	Ethics/Morality	Kindness	Security
Aesthetics/Beauty	Excitement	Leadership	Self-awareness
Authenticity	Exploring	Learning	Self-care
Authority	Fairness	Listening	Self-discipline
Autonomy	Faith	Love	Self-esteem
Balance	Family	Loyalty	Self-sufficiency
Challenge	Financial security	Meaning	Service to others
Commitment	Flexibility	Moderation	Sex
Communication	Forgiveness	Nature	Social status
Community	Freedom	Nurturing	Socialization
Companionship	Friendship	Nutrition	Space
Compassion	Frugality	Obligation	Spirituality
Competition	Fun	Parenting	Spontaneity
Conformity	Generosity	Passion	Stability
Connection	Global responsibility	Peace	Structure
Conservation	Gratification	Perfection	Supportability
Contentment	Happiness	Personal growth	Survival
Contribution	Harmony	Play	Teaching
Control/Power	Health/Fitness	Pleasure	Teamwork
Cooperation	Helping	Pride	Time freedom
Creativity	Home	Prosperity/Wealth	Tolerance
Cultural heritage	Honesty	Purpose	Tradition
Curiosity	Humility	Quietness	Trust
Dependability	Humor	Reciprocity	Truth
Diversity/Differences	Idealism	Recognition	Variety
Duty	Influence	Relationship	Wholeness
Education	Independence	Religious faith	Wisdom
Efficiency	Integrity	Respect	Wonder
Elegance/Grace	Intimacy	Responsibility	Work

Figure 2.1   Examples of core values.

1. Highlight or place a star next to the values in Figure 2.1 that reverberate with you. At least a couple dozen should stand out to you.
2. Next, rank the 10 most important values to you, from most important to the least.
3. Have your partner rank these values for themselves.
4. Finally, take your newly ranked lists and discuss them together. One-by-one, state what each core value is and what

it looks like to you. Share examples of times that each of your core values have been protected or violated. Give your partner tips for helping you maintain balance, without regular violation of your core values.

For example, I would remark:

"My top core value is control. Before I became a stepmom and co-parent, I was single and in control of everything in my life, from what time I awoke and went to sleep, to where or what I'd eat for dinner, to how clean my house was. I recognize that some of these will inevitably be out of my control when entering into a relationship, but there are ways you could help me too. It would mean so much to me if we could discuss changes to our schedule before you agree to them with your ex. I would then feel like I have more control over my schedule, if I could discuss them with you instead of being told that things have changed."

"Honesty is really important to me. When my stepson lies about doing his chores, it triggers me. I recognize that it's probably pretty typical for a child his age to want to avoid chores. But when the dishonesty goes unaddressed or unpunished, it really leaves me feeling provoked. It would mean a lot to me if there were consequences for breaking the house rules every time. That consistency with honesty would really help me to feel protected."

"Structure is one of my core values. I find this is most applicable when I'm thinking about schedules. I like having a consistent schedule and structure in my days. It helps me to thrive. I'd really like us to have a consistent after-school routine, which I think will set us all up for success in the long run. Can we try out having regular dinner times, consistent bedtimes, and designated couple time daily and see how it goes? We don't have to be so regimented that we're scheduling every little thing, and we can certainly have some flexibility. But just having those three things scheduled on the calendar at about the same time daily would help me out a lot."

This exercise serves a few different purposes:

1. **It gives you a deeper understanding of why triggering events are so upsetting.**

   Let's use an example that I've heard many times before. Imagine your partner arrives home from work, shares about their day, and then casually mentions that the other parent signed your stepson up for T-ball. Your blood instantly begins to boil, as you have a physical response to the news. Your partner, however, doesn't understand why you're so upset–you love your stepson, and you love baseball. In fact, you two had just discussed signing him up for T-ball a couple of weeks before! Let's reflect. The other parent's unilateral decision to sign your stepson up for sports might be triggering because you have a core value of control, and don't want someone else to dictate how you'll be spending your Tuesday evenings and Saturday mornings. You want to be the one making the decisions that affect you–not someone else, and especially not your partner's ex.

   Understanding the root of a trigger takes an overwhelming problem without a solution, and converts it into a much more clear and manageable one.

2. **It gives you a deeper understanding of your partner and why they act the way that they do.**

   I used to get so frustrated when Kevin, my husband, would agree to things just to keep the peace with his ex. It often felt like he was choosing her over me when he made those decisions. It wasn't until I asked him about his core values when I learned that harmony was one of his top values, and I began to see why he was choosing not to disrupt the peace with his ex.

   When I found myself uncertain about why he was making a certain decision, or was affected by a situation, I would review the list of his top core values and identify the likely culprit. It helped us work through conflict in a more efficient and respectful manner.

It has also equipped me with powerful knowledge to better protect him from violations of his core values. It helped me approach conversations in a way that reduced the likelihood of triggering him.

3. **It gives your partner a deeper understanding of you and how to best protect you.**

Once Kevin began understanding that I value communication, he learned that it's best to overcommunicate (as if there's such a thing) with me, rather than risk under-communicating. He told me about every conversation he had with his ex and his lawyer and shared his philosophies on parenting and his dreams for the future. Together, we devoted a lot of time to developing our skills for communicating through conflict.

I eventually learned that I didn't need all that communication. Yet, knowing he was an open book when I need him to be, kept me from being triggered by a lack of communication.

4. **It provides you with new vocabulary to discuss triggering events.**

Your partner likely doesn't have the same exact core values as you. That's perfectly normal! They do have their own set of core values, however, and they know what it feels like to have those core values violated. So, they can understand what it feels like when you have yours violated.

Your partner's core values may not include honesty, but they can reflect when they hear you say, "Babe, my core value of honesty is being triggered right now. I need to take a break alone to read or take a bath for a bit. Can you please address the dishonesty with my stepdaughter before I return? I would really appreciate it." Now, your partner knows you've been triggered, recognizes what that feels like, and can take steps to protect you.

The next time that an event provokes you, reflect on which of your core values is being violated. What do you need to occur in order to feel that your core value has been restored? Communicate these needs to your partner, so they can support you in reclaiming peace.

House Rules and Family Meetings

"Kids need structure to feel safe, to know what to expect, and to have a sense of control over their world."[12]
                    – Dr. Becky Kennedy, author of *Good Inside*

When I first moved in with Kevin, we didn't have hard-and-fast rules that were clearly defined. We thought we knew the rules and had properly communicated them to my stepdaughter, Krista. Yet, in reality, our feedback given when she did something "wrong" only made her worry that she was going to make mistakes and get in trouble.

It was up to us to clearly define and communicate those expectations, so she didn't feel like she was aiming for a moving target. No matter how clear you think you've been ("Kristen, I tell them to put their dishes in the dishwasher every day!"), I can guarantee that if you've not had a family meeting about the house rules and posted them where everyone can read them, then your stepchildren aren't as aligned with the rules as you want them to be.

Creating house rules in stepfamilies (and all families) is a way to bring organization and calm to situations that can feel out of control. It's why one of the very first things you will do for a Quick Win is to establish and communicate clear expectations. House rules help create structure and clarity for all family members.

But before you can begin implementing house rules, you must first empathize with your stepchildren. If your stepchildren live in two homes, they likely have different rules and expectations in their other home. When they enter your home, you often expect them to remember your house norms, routines, and rules. It's not always that simple for them to "flip the switch" from one house to the other, however.

Just a few weeks ago, my stepdaughter, Krista, returned to our home after a week at her mom's home and asked me where the forks were kept because she couldn't remember. She lives at our home 50% of the time, yet couldn't remember which drawer the forks were in. Where the silverware is located is just one small thing to remember, so imagine how hard it is to keep up with all the different expectations in both homes.

HOUSE RULES CREATE A SAFE AND PREDICTABLE SPACE FOR EVERYONE

I empathize with our partners who struggle to set firm boundaries or implement too many rules for fear of losing their child's love. Yet when implemented correctly, house rules only serve to benefit your family. Children need structure in their lives, and they look to their parents to provide it.

When a child knows the limits of acceptable behavior, they can thrive within them. But without clear expectations or structure, a child might feel uncertain or overwhelmed. By providing them with well-defined house rules, they don't need to guess what we require of them. They don't have to assume what our expectations are. They'll know them, understand them, and can respect them.

Further, the creation of house rules gives the couple an opportunity to reach an agreement on expectations. Have you ever felt annoyed cleaning up a child's mess *again*? Or maybe you've felt disrespected when your stepson pulled his phone out during dinner? Both of these moments ultimately will snowball into a big heaping pile of resentment toward your partner and the child. And I don't have to tell you that resentment is bad for relationships.

Mitigate resentment, drama, and avoidable arguments by agreeing on expectations from the onset. It's much easier to have a civil, respectful conversation about each other's core values and home culture needs when there isn't an issue present. Don't wait until after someone feels disrespected and emotions are high to have this crucial conversation. Protect your relationship and your family beforehand, even if it means embracing discomfort to reach an agreement.

Prioritizing this productive conversation *prevents* countless conversations down the road when someone's expectations aren't met.

Recognizing and Communicating Expectations

Perhaps the single greatest cause of conflict in stepcouples is unmet expectations. When one (or both) of you expects things to happen a certain way and reality plays out another, it can result in frustration, resentment, and distance in your relationship. When you can learn to recognize your expectations earlier and voice them more frequently to your partner, you'll actively mitigate future conflict.

Often, we don't realize that we had expectations until they go unmet. But the more often you practice acknowledging them, the easier it will become to recognize them in the future. In your daily life, your expectations can reveal themselves in so many ways that you might not be able to anticipate them all ahead of time. I remember preparing for our honeymoon and telling Kevin I was really looking forward to disconnecting for a week–no phones, no email, and so on. He was understandably shocked, because as a dad, he wanted to be in contact with his daughter while we were away. Luckily, we were able to discuss this expectation ahead of time and align our expectations and actions. Can you imagine what a minefield that would've been if, while on our honeymoon, I was triggered every time I saw my husband on his phone? Yikes!

Realizing that you won't prevent every expectation misalignment, it does help if you tackle some of the larger, more common topics that you can anticipate arising in your blended family. A few of the big topics I think you to need to be sure you reflect on and share with your partner are: expectations on parenting styles, house rules, household duties, and alone time as a couple; what respect looks like to you; what your stepmom role should look like; and how you'll split time between your families of origin during holidays. Unmet expectations on any of these topics will cause a disagreement at best, and resentment at worst.

HOUSE RULES HELP THE STEPMOM FEEL HER GRIEVANCES ARE BEING ACKNOWLEDGED AND ADDRESSED

Throughout this book, we'll revisit the topic of validation repeatedly. If a stepmom's partner can learn nothing else from me, I hope it's to say three life-changing words: "I hear you." Stepmoms need to feel heard and understood. This is nonnegotiable.

A stepmom deserves to feel at peace in her home. When her partner is willing to collaborate on and enforce house rules, she feels like her partner hears her, sees her, and wants to protect her. This is all any stepmom really, truly needs.

HOUSE RULES PROTECT STEPPARENTS

Taking it a step further, house rules not only help a stepmom feel seen, but they also help protect her. When a house rule is set by the original parent, a stepmom isn't "the bad guy" for enforcing the parent's rules. It relieves some of the burden and blame, which benefits the stepmom-stepchild relationship. It shifts the narrative from "My stepmom is so mean and has so many rules!" to "Ugh, I don't like that rule my parent made."

Stepmoms already have enough working against them; they don't also need to be the ones responsible for the rules that tell a stepchild what they can and cannot do.

HOW TO SUCCESSFULLY IMPLEMENT RULES

The next few pages introduce a step-by-step list for creating and successfully implementing house rules for your stepfamily.

1. The parents should discuss the rules that they desire ahead of time

Keep the list fairly short; include no more than seven rules. Consider your core values and nonnegotiables and then set your house rules accordingly to protect them.

One thing you should not consider: the other parents' rules in their home. How the other parent chooses to run their home should have no bearing on how you choose to run yours. You might be thinking, "But Kristen! You told me it's like they're flipping a switch between the two homes. … Shouldn't I try to make that easier for them by aligning rules?" Nope! You should set rules that support and protect the core values of you and your partner.

Yes, it's difficult for kids to adjust sometimes. But it's absolutely possible for them to switch between different rules and norms in different places. Think of it this way: Even kids in nuclear families follow different rules at school than they do at home.

Here are some examples of house rules or expectations to get you started:

- ◆ Treat each other with respect.
- ◆ Always tell the truth.
- ◆ We are all on one team.
- ◆ If you mess it up, clean it up.

- No excuses.
- Ask permission first.
- No phones at the dinner table.

2. Get your kids' input on the house rules

Your children don't get to veto rules you have set, but they might want to give feedback on the rules you've presented or propose their own.

For example, when we first began setting our house rules, my stepdaughter, Krista, asked if we could set a one-hour period where no one was on their devices. Listening to her feedback helped her feel heard and resulted in a new rule about screen-free time for our household.

3. Post the rules somewhere everyone can see them

Everyone in the household should know, understand, and follow the rules. Keeping in mind that everyone leads busy lives with work, school, errands, and other responsibilities, make the house rules easily accessible. Posting your rules in the main part of the home ensures that the list of rules isn't a "discuss it once and forget about it two days later" conversation.

Remembering the rules will be easy if you write them down and post them together as a family! One of my coaching clients made a big deal out of this process. Everyone in her family got to pick out their favorite color marker and write one of the rules down on a poster.

4. Review your rules on transition days

Want to make transition days, or the days the children switch homes, happier and a smoother experience for all? Create consistent traditions so your stepkids know what to expect. When kids know what to expect, they are calmer and happier. (We'll dive into this in greater detail in Chapter 8.) As part of your transition day ritual, take a moment to review the house rules with your stepchildren. You can do this over your first meal with them or in the car after pickup.

This isn't a foolproof solution—just a helpful tool. Even though it helps when you review the rules at the onset of your custodial period, still be prepared to remind them of the rules throughout your time together.

5. Be a good role model

Follow the house rules yourself to set a good example for the kids, and to set the right tone for the home. The kids will then follow your lead.

Once the rules are posted, they need to be strictly enforced … for everyone! If a rule dictates no screens during dinner in your house, parents should be following that rule as well. Children will be confused (and likely resentful) if parents aren't held to the same expectations. For example, if the kids aren't allowed to watch a TV show during Tuesday's dinner, they won't understand the exception when parents are allowed, during dinner, to cheer on their favorite team during Thursday Night Football. In response, the children might begin to show a similar disregard–or disdain–for the house rules. As stepmoms, we know how much it sucks when there's a double standard. These are *house* rules and not "just kid" rules after all!

Part of the responsibility in setting the tone as the leader is enforcing the rules, which leads me to my final point.

6. Be prepared to enforce the rules

Have patience and exercise empathy but issue consequences when necessary.

As a rule of thumb, consequences should include either taking away something the child likes or adding something the child doesn't like.

Examples of the former include taking away an iPad, losing the privilege to play with friends after school, or no longer going to the swimming pool as planned on a hot summer day.

Examples of the latter include adding chores, having the child write an apology letter, or having the child watch a younger sibling while you prepare dinner.

I advise as parents that you set aside time early in the relationship to brainstorm various consequences for your children. Aim for a few of each type of consequence per child. Then, when a rule is broken, you'll have a prepared list to pull from and won't have to come up with something on the spot.

I do not recommend having a set punishment for each infraction.

A reliable, consistent punishment gives the child the opportunity to weigh the value of breaking the rule against the punishment they know they'll receive.

For example, a teenager might decide the advantage of sneaking their phone into their room is worth the risk of getting caught breaking the house rule and getting stuck with laundry duty for a week.

My stepdaughter is a very good kid and rarely gets in trouble. Because of this long track record, Kevin hesitates to punish her when she does, inevitably, break a house rule. When this happens, I remind him of the importance of house rules and encourage him to stay consistent with enforcement.

THE IMPORTANCE OF FAMILY MEETINGS

A family meeting is exactly what it sounds like but is less boring and draconian than it probably sounds. It's a designated time for the entire family to gather and discuss issues in a roundtable format, led by your partner, the original parent. Ideally, you'd have these meetings on a recurring schedule, but ad hoc family meetings are better than none.

If you haven't hosted a family meeting before, ensure that everyone knows they aren't in trouble. Sometimes, family meetings get a bad rap. But I want them to be a positive space for your family to be comfortable communicating with each other honestly and openly.

A family meeting is the ideal setting for presenting the compiled list of house rules to the rest of the household for the first time. You'll want everyone's undivided attention and a forum where everyone has the opportunity to speak (and not just be spoken at).

To start, kick the meeting off with a fun icebreaker. Try a Minute To Win It game or another simple game like Two Truths and a Lie or Would You Rather. Next, establish expectations for the meeting: Everyone has a right to share their opinions and is encouraged to do so, no talking over one another, and so on. After setting the ground rules, ensure everyone gets a turn to speak about whatever they would like. I tend to start with the easy emotionless topic of the family calendar. I will share what's upcoming for next month: the custody schedule, birthdays or other important occasions, vacations, and school events.

I highly recommend having your partner take the lead on any parenting or corrective conversations. Children receive these messages from their original parents better than they do from their stepparents. In your first meeting, your partner should clearly present the established list of house rules and provide examples. They should then extend their authority to you very directly. For example, my husband, Kevin, would say something like, "As my wife, Kristen is an extension of me. If she says to do something or enforces a rule, it's the same thing as if I said it." It's critical that children hear this very directly communicated from their original parent.

Family meetings may feel uncomfortable or too formal at first, but the more often you gather, the more comfortable they'll become. In my family, we're at a point now that my stepdaughter, Krista, will even call family meetings when she wants to discuss something. Everyone in my family feels heard (validated) in this space.

Your New Daily Routine

"We are what we repeatedly do. Excellence, then, is not an act, but a habit."[13]

— Aristotle, ancient Greek philosopher

Stepmomming is one of the most overwhelming things that I've ever experienced. It can overwhelm you physically, financially, emotionally, and beyond. My entire goal with this book is to equip you with the tools to make your relationship sustainable and fulfilling. If your relationship is going to go the distance and become a source of joy for you, you'll need to develop healthy daily habits. I don't want this to be a time-consuming process for you (it must be sustainable), but I wouldn't recommend these four practices if I didn't believe they were critically necessary for your mental health and the viability of your relationship.

HABIT #1: KISS YOUR PARTNER EVERY SINGLE DAY

I'm hoping to get your buy-in early on these recommendations by making kissing your partner the first daily habit on the practices list. It doesn't need to be a full make-out session, although it can be. A chaste, closed-lip kiss will do. This habit should be extremely easy to accomplish, and it's likely something you're already doing. But if you've felt disconnected from your partner recently–maybe you're in a busy phase, or perhaps a resentful one–you might be forgetting to do this essential ritual. Connecting with your partner is nonnegotiable, however.

If your partner isn't the absolute best person that you've ever met, don't put yourself through the challenges of stepfamily life. Call it quits and cut your losses. You have my full permission to do so. However, if your partner is, indeed, as incredible as you believe they are, remind yourself of it as often as you can. They're the only person who can make all the drama and the challenges worth it.

HABIT #2: AFFIRM YOURSELF DAILY

An affirmation is a proven method of rewiring your brain.[14] When you change your individual thoughts, you change your thought pattern. When negativity is the main message in your brain, you're left feeling unhappy and unfulfilled. If you can rewire your brain to think positively about yourself and your situation with positive affirmation, I'm certain you'll be in a better place afterward.

I want you to choose an affirmation from the list given in Figure 2.2 or create your own and place it somewhere you'll see it daily. Write it down on a sticky note and place it on your car's rearview mirror. Use a dry erase marker and write it on your bathroom mirror. In your phone, set a recurring daily reminder of your affirmation. Just write it somewhere that you'll see it every day.

The affirmation you choose should speak directly to your biggest struggle or insecurity. It should be the reminder that you need. If I were your personal stepmom coach, what permission would you need to hear from me daily? Your response should be what you select as your daily affirmation.

If you're struggling with feeling guilty for communicating your needs, your affirmation should be something similar to, "I deserve to take up space and feel comfortable in my own home." If you're grieving the fact that your partner experienced many of their firsts with another partner, remind yourself, "Our relationship is special, and my partner chooses me today and every day."

Do daily affirmation reminders seem a bit silly or inconsequential to you? Sure, they do. ... I get it. But again, I wouldn't ask you to do

AFFIRMATIONS

Choose an affirmation to recite to yourself daily. The list below will
give you inspiration, but you're welcome to create your own.

1. I am an intelligent, beautiful woman with a kind soul and a gentle heart.
2. I am invincible. I can handle any challenge that comes my way.
3. I am exactly where I'm supposed to be.
4. I am a role model worthy of my (step)children's admiration.
5. I am my partner's first choice, and the love of their life.
6. I forgive those who have hurt me in the past and will move forward peacefully.
7. I am greater than the negative thoughts, words, and actions.
8. My relationship is stronger and deeper today than it was yesterday.
9. Many people see me and recognize my worth. I am loved.
10. I have many friends and family. I am blessed by these relationships.
11. I fully accept who I am.
12. I am confident in who I am as a woman, parent, and partner.
13. I am worthy of love and happiness.
14. I am not a victim of my circumstances.
15. I am in control of my own destiny.
16. I choose happiness today.
17. I am grateful for my life.
18. I am filled with hope.
19. I will stand by my decisions. I am a logical, methodical decision-maker.
20. I accept my partner for who they are.
21. I accept my (step)children for who they are.
22. I love every cell in my body.
23. I am an incredible (step)mom.
24. I am a wonderful partner.
25. I am strong, physically and mentally.
26. I have a beautiful mind.
27. I will rise above the conflict.
28. I have great ideas and make useful contributions.
29. I am proud of myself.
30. I am enough.

Figure 2.2   Sample affirmations.

this if I didn't really believe that they can make a massive difference
in your life.

HABIT #3: JOURNAL YOUR INNER THOUGHTS

As a recovering overthinker, I had an incredibly challenging time getting out of my own head in my more overwhelming days as a new
stepmom. I'd find myself consumed with thoughts of my husband's

ex and my stepmom role. The following big thoughts were always at the forefront of my mind:

- Why did she unexpectedly serve us paperwork to modify the custody agreement? What is the court process going to look like? How much is this going to cost us? WHY?
- What is my place in our family? Where do I fit in? Am I doing ok? Do they deserve better than I can offer?
- Will I ever feel special to my husband if I'm his second wife, and he's already experienced all his "firsts" with someone else?
- Can I do this for the rest of my life?

These less-significant-but-ever-present thoughts were there too:

- Will Krista like the way that I cook pasta? Will it be as good as her mom's?
- I'd love to have a girl's day and go with Krista to the nail salon. But will her mom be upset?
- Will there be any conflict at the custody exchange today?
- Why don't any of the cute clothes we buy Krista get brought back home?
- What did that text mean?
- Is the ex talking about us poorly at the other home?
- How will the ex's new partner integrate into these dynamics?
- How will Krista's life be affected by her new stepsister?
- How does our sex life compare to the one he had with his first wife?
- Will his ex be at the Open House this evening? Will their daughter want to show them things first, leaving me on the outside looking in?

My brain was like a prison with a seemingly never-ending supply of questions and anxious thoughts about my stepfamily dynamics and everything that is or was possibly going wrong.

Then, I learned about the Morning Pages journaling exercise: "three pages of longhand, stream of consciousness writing done first thing in the morning," a practice detailed in *The Artist's Way*.[15] You can either stick to the original format, or if you prefer, wake up and set a 10-minute timer before you begin. Then, write whatever comes to mind–no censoring or judging your thoughts. This journal is only for you and will not be shared with anyone else, so simply write what comes to mind. Eject those intrusive thoughts out of your brain and onto paper. Write about your frustration and anger. Giving your anxious thoughts a place on the page helps you acknowledge them and release their grip.

When you begin your day by expelling your concerns, you open brain space for other, more productive thoughts. Sometimes, all we need to do to feel relief from worry is to verbalize it. If you use this journaling exercise to give those thoughts a voice, you've given them the attention they need to be dismissed, opening time and space for more important or fulfilling thoughts.

You're also actively processing the worries you've listed while journaling, so they won't exist long without resolution. Use this journal time to break down how you want to respond to the ex's latest attack, how you'd like to reflect and redefine your stepmom role to eliminate resentment, or to really evaluate what was so triggering about your partner's comment the prior night.

Instead of enabling your thoughts to hold you captive in an endless worrisome thought loop, you can take ownership of them and get out of the worry spiral. It simply takes 10 minutes and a pen and paper. If you're worried about someone else reading your notes, you can always shred, toss, or burn your notes after you're done (which is the most cathartic, in my opinion). Another option is to journal electronically on your phone or computer. Don't let the fear of someone else discovering your thoughts keep you from processing them.

HABIT #4: PRACTICE GRATITUDE

For the final daily activity, I want you to incorporate the practice of gratitude into your routine. I tend to lump gratitude in with meditation, manifestation, and other practices that life coaches swear by but seem superficial. But the reality is, when you rewire your brain for gratitude, your entire perspective shifts. I know your hesitation. I can practically see your eye roll. But try it for just one month, and if you really don't feel it's making a difference, you can stop.

During my senior year of college, my school offered a class on gratitude. It fell under a category I required credit for, so I took it. I thought it was a bit silly, but as a double major with about a thousand extracurricular commitments, I needed an "easy credit." It took only a few weeks before I started to see a difference. My school was located in Southern California, in one of the most expensive zip codes in the nation. One morning while driving to campus, I distinctly remember passing a gas station and being thankful that even though gas prices were high, at least they weren't $5 per gallon. Compared to my mindset before taking the class, I definitely noticed a seismic shift.

When you focus on what you're grateful for, you're less focused on what isn't going according to plan. As a stepmom, you're focused more on your partner and the beautiful love you share–and less on their ex's antics, the mess your stepchildren have made of your home, or any other struggle. You learn to reframe your life and see how good actually overshadows bad.

Figure 2.3 is a stepmom-specific gratitude worksheet that you can use as a template to manifest your gratitude, or you can simply state three things you're grateful for that happened that day. Make these items as specific as possible. You can be grateful to have a roof over your head and a bed to sleep in, but I want your three items to be specifically related to the day you've had. Examples include: "I'm grateful my partner made me coffee," "I'm grateful that traffic was light this evening," and "I'm grateful that my stepson was in a good mood when he got home from school." Some days it might feel like a stretch to identify three specific items. Others, it will be easy for you to list a dozen. Regardless, continue to practice gratitude each and every day, and you'll discover the different lens through which you'll view your stepfamily.

If you want to take it a step further at some point, write a letter expressing your gratitude to your partner, your stepchild, or your stepchild's other parent (only if you are on good terms with them). Give the letter to them, or if you want what co-authors of *Burnout: The Secret to Unlocking the Stress Cycle*, Drs. Amelia and Emily Nagoski call a "super-burst of gratitude … [that] can boost your well-being for a full month, or even up to three months," read the letter aloud to the recipient.[16] Gratitude is directly related to your health and can make you feel immensely better about your life.

With these Quick Wins and new habits under your belt, you're hopefully feeling motivated to make larger, more meaningful

GRATITUDE

For each gratitude category, identify something specific you're grateful for that happened in the last 24 hours. Instead of being grateful for your partner generally, you might be grateful they let you sleep in this morning. Then, celebrate three wins from the day.

TODAY'S GRATITUDE

my partner

the kids

our custody/co-parenting situation

a challenge or trial

my talents & strengths

TODAY'S WINS

1

2

3

Figure 2.3   Stepmom–specific gratitude worksheet.

changes in your life. We'll spend the rest of the book working through what I call the Forever Formula for Stepmoms, my six-step foundation-building curriculum that will teach you how to live a sustainable life of peace and happiness as a stepmom. It's a big promise, and I plan to deliver. So, let's dive in!

CHAPTER 3

The Forever Formula for Stepmoms

The bulk of this book will walk you through the six steps to reclaim peace in your life. I lovingly refer to it as the Forever Formula for Stepmoms. Each step builds off the previous one as a foundation, so do not move ahead to the next step if you're still working through the current one. I understand the temptation to rush this life-changing transformation along, but a sustainable, long-lasting metamorphosis doesn't work that way. Evolving requires your time and full attention.

The six steps of the Forever Formula for Stepmoms are:

1. Develop an Attitude of Self-Worth
2. Define an Authentic Role
3. Balance Self-Fulfillment
4. Cultivate an Unshakable Relationship
5. Command Confident Control
6. Seek Validating Support

I thoughtfully and intentionally designated the steps in their given order. So, while I respect your need for control or your desire to redefine your role, be patient and work through the steps in order, fully. It will be worth the wait, I promise. You'll be better primed to reclaim control, or to redefine your role, once you've worked through the preceding steps. Remember, this formula is thoughtfully and intentionally designed.

Basic Review of the Six Steps of the Forever Formula

The first step of the Forever Formula for Stepmoms is: Develop an Attitude of Self-Worth. In this step, we'll address your struggles with insecurities of any type: second-spouse insecurities (discussed in greater detail in the next chapter), wondering if your family deserves better, or imposter syndrome. You'll leave this step confident in the value you add to your family and the knowledge that you are a great stepmom.

The second step of the Forever Formula for Stepmoms is: Define an Authentic Role. In this step, we'll address guilt and other counterproductive motivators to how you show up in your family. We'll explore your beliefs and values to help you clearly define a stepmom role of which you can feel proud of and thrive within.

The third step of the Forever Formula for Stepmoms is: Balance Self-Fulfillment. This role will suck every bit of time and energy you have, if you allow it to do so. We'll explore why so many stepmoms experience an "identity crisis" and teach you how to find yourself again. We'll also address burnout–why it happens, how to avoid it, and how to recover when it inevitably sneaks in again. Rediscover yourself again in this step!

The fourth step of the Forever Formula for Stepmoms is: Cultivate an Unshakable Relationship. Your partner is the reason that you're a stepmom, and if that relationship is impaired, the rest of the family dynamic will be as well. We'll work through a variety of tools to help your relationship with your partner become as strong as possible. Dare I say, unshakable?

The fifth step of the Forever Formula for Stepmoms, and often the most anticipated, is: Command Confident Control. Here, we finally explore setting boundaries, taking back control from a co-parent who doesn't respect them, and the mindset shift you need to stop feeling like blended family life is happening *to* you. It is possible to have control as a stepmom. You don't have to feel like the custody schedule, your stepchildren, the other parent, and your partner are running your life.

The sixth and final step of the Forever Formula for Stepmoms is: Seek Validating Support. I can coach you with every single mindset tool I know, and there will likely still be things that happen in your stepmom life that make you think "The audacity!" or "Are you kidding me!" When that happens, you need a stepmom friend who understands why it's upsetting and can validate that experience for you. This person understands you didn't know what you were signing up for, and they've got your back. In this section, I'll share my favorite ways to find new stepmom friends.

The Top Three Priorities for a Stepmom

I bet you've noticed, the first step (and several others) is entirely centered on you, the stepmom. You must be your top priority in your family. In any given situation, your decision must reflect what would give you the most peace. Maybe it sounds selfish or immature but think about it this way: If you're unhappy or frustrated–or worse, resentful–there will be a trickle effect that affects the rest of the family. Your frustration will be taken out on your stepchildren. Your partner will bear the brunt of your resentment. The entire family will sense that you're in a bad mood, and it will place a damper on the rest of the day. Frankly, after years of working with stepmoms, I've seen many stubborn clients try it their way; it doesn't work. It's why I'm sharing with you the exact path to a sustainable, fulfilling stepmom life you love. Trust it!

The second priority for a stepmom, after she achieves peace of mind, is her relationship with her partner. If you feel at peace and are then faced with another decision, choose the option that most protects or benefits you and your partner. I might sound like a broken record, but you're only a stepmom because of your partner. You must nurture and prioritize that relationship for it to succeed.

Finally, the third priority is your family. Once you feel at peace internally and your relationship feels solid, only then can you make a decision that benefits or protects your family. If you or your relationship aren't at peace, then making a decision for your children or stepchildren can contribute to resentment or other negative feelings.

If you listen to nothing else that I have to say, I hope you will embrace your three top priorities, in that order. This mindset shift helps you protect your personal peace when a member of your blended family life threatens to disrupt it. You deserve peace of mind and harmony in your home.

Stepmom's Hierarchy of Priorities

1. Your peace of mind
2. Your relationship
3. Your family

Each of the following chapters explains one step of the Forever Formula in great detail. In each chapter, you'll find real stepmom stories, research-backed tools and strategies, and activities to implement what you'll learn along the way. As I've mentioned, this book was intentionally designed in its designated order. Do the activities and master the lessons in their given order before moving on to the next chapter. The stronger your foundation, the better your quality of life will be. I know it sounds dramatic, but it's true.

CHAPTER 4

Develop an Attitude of Self-Worth

Welcome to step 1 of the Forever Formula! This chapter focuses entirely on self-confidence and self-worth. Before you can improve your relationships with others in your stepfamily dynamic, you must first feel fully confident in what you bring to your family.

We begin with a deep dive into the importance of mourning the loss of the future and family structure of which you dreamed. You didn't dream of becoming a stepmom. There were no custody schedules or stepchildren in your vision for your family as a little girl. Until you've grieved the loss of that dream, you'll continue to be triggered by all the ways your current life varies from that dream. Allowing yourself to mourn and process that loss opens your heart to be fully present and engaged in your real, perfectly imperfect, blended family.

After you've fully mourned the loss, you'll be ready to tackle other barriers to self-worth as a stepmom. We'll work through the insecurities many stepmoms face, knowing their partner was with someone else and has experienced many major milestones for the first time with them. I'll share with you the six reminders that I needed to hear when I was overwhelmed with these insecurities in my early stepmom days. You are your partner's first choice, and you will walk away from this chapter and its corresponding activities confident in that fact.

Next, you'll receive an impassioned lecture from your favorite stepmom coach, encouraging you to recognize that you are an incredible stepmom. We'll address your feeling like an out-sider and the concern that your family deserves better when you struggle in your role. In order to be a great stepmom, you must believe that you're a great stepmom. This is the imperative first step in developing a foundation conducive to lasting peace and happiness.

Mourning the Loss of the Future You Envisioned

"You can't start the next chapter of your life if you keep rereading the last one."[17]
> – Michael McMillan, best-selling author, speaker, and innovation and creativity consultant

Kevin and I had been dating for about six months when he bought a new house. Being the ever-pleasant partner that I am, I offered to unpack his things and help him and Krista get settled. Fully self-aware, I knew I would be triggered to find anything from his past relationship. Even his ex's handwriting on some of the boxes was enough to set me off.

I chose to help with an innocuous looking enough selection of boxes marked as movies for the living room. I started unpacking and sorting between adult movies and children's movies before I saw it … their wedding video.

It stopped me dead in my tracks, and I had to get away.

I told Kevin I needed to run to the grocery store, and I got in the car, called my mom, and bawled like a baby.

It was then that I started the grieving process.

Growing up, you likely dreamed of getting married, maybe having kids, and growing old with the love of your life. You probably didn't factor in an ex-partner, stepchildren, a custody schedule, and court battles. In your dream, your partner wasn't divorced, you had the vision just like you sang on the playground: "First comes love, then comes marriage, then comes a baby in the baby carriage …" That reality isn't something you can sweep under the rug. Your vision for your future felt so very real to you before you met your partner who didn't perfectly align with your dream.

This path you've chosen is far more complex than the life you dreamed of. Things aren't going to be as easy as they would be for couples without the extra factors of children, ex-partners, and custody agreements. You didn't have the same honeymoon period, the late nights out alone without responsibility, or the autonomy over your schedule for last-minute vacations. You skipped past the tiny one-bedroom apartment straight to a life with kids, shuttling between school and soccer games. On top of that, you have the stepmom stigmas, double standards, and impossible expectations to manage.

Accepting that your future appears differently than the one you'd dreamed of is a critical first step. You can't fully move forward until you grieve and accept your new reality.

Until you have fully mourned the loss of the life you thought you would live, you will be triggered by reminders of that reality, like I was with the wedding video. Those little triggers can grow into mounting resentment that can consume you. Instead, recognize and accept that things are different. Different doesn't have to mean worse, but it is still fundamentally *different*.

As long as you're holding onto the image of how things should have looked, you'll always compare your reality to that image. And every time something new comes up, reminding you that you're not living the dream you once dreamt, know that you will get triggered again. It's time to put away the old dream and open yourself up fully to the beautiful new dream ahead.

Mourn the loss of that easier life, the way you wanted things to be, and allow yourself to feel the full depth of that loss. Then, once you have given yourself that time to grieve, focus on all the reasons you have chosen this life. Remember all the reasons your partner is worth the extra effort, the co-parenting or kid drama, and the "different." Remind yourself why you said yes!

Once you have worked through this process and mourned the loss of the life you thought you'd live–the future you thought you'd have–you can fully and truly live in the moment and look forward to the future with your chosen partner.

Activity: Mourn Your Loss

Mourn the loss of the future you thought you'd have. You had dreams and a vision for what your future marriage and/or family would look like, and your current reality differs from that vision. Allow yourself the opportunity to grieve that loss.

To practically mourn the loss, find a quiet space for visualization. Close your eyes and picture the future you once imagined. Explore that life. What do you see? Are you and your partner traveling kid-free? Have you accomplished certain career goals before deciding to have children? Do you even see children in that dream? Now, shift your focus to your present reality and your real family.

Consider the differences. Take a deep breath and notice the feelings that arise when you catalog the differences. Are you angry? Sad? Frustrated? Allow yourself to feel each emotion without censorship or judgment. After you've honored each reaction, ask yourself, "What opportunities exist in this new life that didn't before? How can this be even more beautiful and fulfilling than I imagined?" Allow yourself to explore those possibilities. Honor your feelings and the very real loss you're experiencing, then release it, and focus forward.

Overcoming Second-Spouse Insecurities

> *"Comparison is the fastest way to take all the fun out of life."*[18]
>
> – Jen Sincero, author of *You Are a Badass*

Have you vacationed there with her? Was that the picnic basket you used as a family? Is that somewhere you had date night with her? I used to think (and ask) about Kevin's ex-wife all the time. I didn't want to replicate any memories that he'd had with her, because then I had the ability to pale in comparison. I didn't want to feel second best, so I did my best to avoid situations that resembled anything he had done with his first wife.

Shortly after we moved in together, I arrived home and discovered my then-boyfriend/now-husband had sold another item that we had posted in a Facebook garage sale group. When I asked which item it was, he told me it was the bed that he had shared with his ex-wife. I never knew that item was in our garage; he didn't even ask if I wanted to keep it, just posted it and sold it (I love that man). In that moment, I felt overwhelming relief. It was gone, out of my house.

When I say that I used to think about his ex-wife all the time, it's not an exaggeration. I was constantly overcome with insecurities, the magnitude of which I didn't know I was capable. I'd flip through his old photos on Facebook, and I couldn't even tell you why. I knew it would hurt, but I did it anyway. I found this self-sabotaging need to continue comparing and feeling inadequate. (In retrospect, I was self-sabotaging as a means of control, protecting myself in case he decided he wasn't over that hurt, or he didn't think I was better by comparison.)

I still remember my exact feelings after one of those "comparison" episodes: the pit in my stomach, along with the nausea and uneasiness that had settled in.

These insecurities are called *second-spouse insecurities*. They're any insecurities you might feel as a subsequent partner. Your partner doesn't need to be married to your stepchild's parent, or be married only once before, for these insecurities to possibly apply to your situation.

Don't Ask Questions That You Don't Want to Hear the Answers To

If you're suffering from these insecurities like I did, I encourage you to stop seeking out information you can't unlearn. You can't unsee the photos of them together. You can't unhear your partner telling you stories or other things about their time together. I know you think you want to know, but there's no real reason you need to know.

Your partner admitting they were happy once, detailing their pregnancy or adoption journey, or God-forbid (but yes, it happens) oversharing about their sex life will only serve to haunt you. Stop scrolling their feed. Stop asking questions you don't really want (nay, *need*) to hear the answers to.

THE REALITY OF COMPARISON

Comparison is the killer of joy. When you allow yourself to continue those comparisons, you're robbing yourself of the potential for a sustainable, loving relationship. You aren't giving yourself an opportunity to be happy with your partner and are instead shutting it down before it's allowed a fighting chance.

You are your partner's choice now, not their ex. You! Comparing yourself to them will only hurt you. There's no benefit to doing it. The only satisfaction you'll get is by proving that tiny nasty voice in the back of your mind right. So, stop feeding that voice. You love your partner, or else you wouldn't be here reading this book, seeking advice on how to move past the crippling fear of comparison, right?

I get it. It felt like Kevin had lived an entire life before he met me. He had joined the military, married, had a daughter, made four cross-country moves, and divorced. I was learning his story and how it had shaped him into the man with whom I was falling in love. And every chapter included her. His ex witnessed so much of his life, and she got to be there with him as he grew up. As much as it still embarrasses me to admit it, I was jealous of her.

When it's your first marriage, but your partner has been married before, it can feel like a gut punch to realize that so many of their firsts were shared together. Things that are new and exciting for you aren't new to your partner, which only compounds those jealous feelings. I found myself wondering if this second chance was as exciting for him without the novelty. I questioned if he was secretly pining for his ex. Or worse, I wondered if he'd ever love me as much as he loved her.

If you find yourself heading down this spiral of second-spouse insecurities like I did in those early days, the following six important reminders will help ground you in reality.

REMINDER #1: IF THAT'S WHAT YOUR PARTNER WANTED, THEY'D HAVE IT

Let's start with the most direct point. If your partner wanted their ex (or someone more like them), they'd be fighting for that relationship, not investing in the relationship with you. That relationship didn't work for a reason, and it will always boil down to incompatibility. This is really great news for you! You get to be the compatible one for your partner. You get to be the missing piece that the ex wasn't capable of being.

REMINDER #2: YOUR PARTNER IS A DIFFERENT PERSON TODAY

Your partner has matured from the break-up and custody negotiation process. The person you are with is not the same person their ex was with. Your partner has learned from past experiences and has a much clearer idea of the type of life partner they want now.

You aren't getting their ex's leftovers. Even if their pasts were in sync, you are getting a new-and-improved version of the person their ex once loved, who is perfect today for the person you are today.

REMINDER #3: IF YOU WEREN'T WORTH THE RISK, YOUR PARTNER WOULDN'T TAKE IT

We have arrived at perhaps the biggest "Aha!" realization for me. My husband was devastated by his divorce and the loss of the nuclear family he'd dreamed of having. He wouldn't risk another heartbreak, another financially draining divorce, or another parental split for his daughter, if I wasn't worth that risk. And neither would your partner. You're everything your significant other is looking for in a life partner. You! Not their ex. You are the reward worth every risk, so trust your partner when they tell you this is the relationship they want today and forevermore.

REMINDER #4: YOUR MILESTONES AREN'T ANY LESS SPECIAL

One of my biggest fears after falling in love with someone who'd been married before is worrying that our milestones would be less special for him. He'd already experienced so many of those firsts. How could the second time around be as meaningful? He had already chosen a ring, gotten down on one knee, walked down the aisle, prepared for a baby, went through the birthing process, celebrated anniversaries, and watched his child learn and grow. ... Getting to experience all of that a second time is certainly cool ... but is it equally as special? I was doubtful.

So, I did what any good Sociology major would do, and I conducted my own research! I polled dozens of people in second marriages and asked them, "In your second marriage, how have your feelings been different? Do you feel like things have ever been less exciting, because you've already experienced some things for the first time in your first marriage?" Friend, not a single person said yes. No one even tried to skirt around the answer and give me a nonanswer, so they wouldn't have to say yes. I received answer after answer of enthusiastic dissent. Person after person gushed about how it's either just as special–or even more so–because now they're experiencing that event with the right person. Having experienced something before didn't make it any less special to them.

Because I know you're skeptical, here's a sample of just a few of the responses that I received:

- ◆ "I'm more excited this second time. I feel like I really know what love is, and like this is more real than the first one."
- ◆ "Yes, it is very different. I'm happier this time around, even with the challenges we've faced. We're both in our second marriages and recognize that we learned a lot of what not to do in our firsts, so we committed to doing things differently from the very beginning of our relationship. All the changes and differences in this marriage make it undeniably better than our firsts. We're happier, communicate better, tackle things as a team, and are more in love. … Although much of what we have experienced together might not be our "first" in life, I don't think it diminishes our excitement. At least not for me. It's exciting to me to be experiencing things or events with this person I love, my partner."
- ◆ "In my second marriage, I feel like everything is better! I'm not missing out on not having 'firsts,' because they are firsts for us together! I am so much more relaxed and able to enjoy our family and moments together, because I'm not trying so hard to make everything perfect. I wasn't jealous or worried when I was pregnant with our son, because this was our son, together, and the love between us is completely different than the loves we knew before."
- ◆ "I am so grateful for second chances! I feel like we both know what to expect in a marriage (been there, done that), so we can just focus on the now and each other. We are more accepting of [each other's] flaws and limit the expectations."
- ◆ "I look at it this way … I got so much wrong the first time around. This time, I knew what I was looking for in a partner. Every first with him is a blessing! My first marriage taught me all the things I didn't want in a marriage/mate!"

REMINDER #5: YOU OFFER SOMETHING SPECIAL AND UNIQUE TO YOUR FAMILY

In my early stepmom days, I often felt like an imposter. Let's try an analogy. Imagine that you were holding a photo of my husband, his ex-wife, and their daughter. And then, you grabbed a pair of scissors and proceeded to cut his ex out of the photo when they got divorced.

What if, when Kevin and I started dating, you took a photo cutout of me and tried to place it in the hole his ex had vacated in the family photo. We were the new family in this house. But … I didn't fit. Of course, I didn't. My photo would never fit in the same hole in the same way that Krista's mom had fit into their family photo.

We are different women with different strengths and different roles. I tried so hard to be version 2.0 of his ex, but it felt forced. It felt like I was going through the motions and failing to do any of those things perfectly, because they weren't authentic to me. I wasn't being true to myself and my strengths and tasks I wanted to do in and for my family.

Instead, recognize the unique value that you add to your family, and play to those strengths. You aren't replacing anyone. You're supplementing the parental system already in place. You don't have to do any of the traditional parenting tasks if you don't want to. You get to show up in whatever ways highlight your talents and add value to your family. This might mean skipping bath time and disciplining your stepchild but instead excelling at story time with your animated character voices and making your stepchild feel special with thoughtful napkin notes packed into their school lunches.

REMINDER #6: LET YOUR PARTNER'S WORD BE THEIR BOND

I'm not (too) ashamed to admit that I sought a lot of validation when I was struggling with these insecurities. I would ask Kevin questions like, "I know you never wanted a divorce, but knowing what you know now about our relationship, would you still choose to divorce and find me?" I wanted to know I wasn't his second choice, the runner-up.

Yet, when he would assure me that I wasn't a consolation, I justified away his answers. I didn't take his words for their face value, so I didn't receive the validation I was seeking, and he was offering. One day, after I pushed back on his answer, Kevin pulled me to look him directly in the eyes and said, "I will not lie to you. I will not say something untrue to make you feel better. Let my word be my bond." It was a powerful moment for us. When you can reflect on all the ways your partner has shown and told you that your relationship is more special with a lens of truth, it can make a world of difference.

LOOKING FORWARD AND ACTIVITIES

Don't look back at what your partner has shared. Look ahead at the life you get to share with your partner; it's a much brighter future. The next time you find yourself spiraling and jealous of the ex and the relationship your partner and their ex shared before you, remind yourself of these six important facts. You are worthy of this love and happiness, sweet stepmom.

This chapter contains a lot of activities to help you move past these second-spouse insecurities that can hold you captive. I encourage you to work through each of them thoroughly if you've had any fears of being second choice or missing out on your partner's firsts.

Activity: Journal About Your Insecurities

The first activity is to journal about your insecurities. It's virtually impossible to resolve second-spouse insecurities as a whole, without understanding the root from where the fears stem. Work your way through these questions, digging deep to understand your fears, and what you need to overcome them and feel confident in what you bring to your relationship.

- What is it that you're truly afraid of? (Examples include that your relationship isn't as special, that you'll always be viewed by comparison, or that your partner will want to go back to their ex-partner.)
- Are you scared that being the second spouse means second choice? Why?
- Why does it hurt so much when you see your partner and their ex together or think about your partner's past with their ex?
- Why are you so threatened by the ex/their relationship?
- What does your partner do that makes you feel inferior?
- What does the ex do that makes you feel inferior?
- What do your stepchildren do that makes you feel inferior?
- You have missed out on some of your partner's firsts. How does it make you feel?
- Why are you holding yourself back from fully jumping into this relationship and trusting your partner?

◆ Why you? (List your positive qualities and what you add to the family.)

◆ What "Aha!" moments did you have as part of this exercise?

Activity: Identify Your Unique Place

The second activity is about reflection. When you look at your step-child's life, how do you fit into the bigger picture? How does everyone work together to raise and support your stepchild?

On the puzzle and its pieces in Figure 4.1, write your stepchild's name in the middle puzzle piece and then fill in each of the influences in their life. (Examples include teachers, coaches, religious leaders, parents and stepparents, and so on.)

If you have more than one stepchild, repeat the activity for each of your stepchildren.

Activity: Start a Validation List

Make a list of all the ways your partner has shown or mentioned that you're their choice now. Not a consolation prize or second best but truly right for them. Continue to add to this list as more things happen. In addition, keep it somewhere easily accessible so you can read through it for validation when you're feeling insecure or unsure.

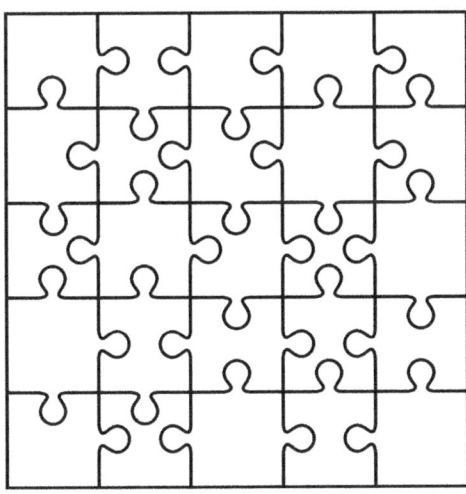

Figure 4.1   Your stepchild's puzzle.

You're a Great Stepmom!

"When we're happy and all in love with ourselves, we can't be bothered with the bullshit (our own or other people's)."[18]
– Jen Sincero, author of *You Are a Badass*

It's important that you know you are where you're supposed to be, and you're a great stepmom. You're whole already. You aren't lacking or failing as a stepmom. This book is here to provide you with the education and tools to master stepfamily life and create peace, no matter what stepfamily life throws at you. You are strong, loving, and devoted. You wouldn't be here reading this book if you weren't. That simple act tells me you are a great stepmom, and that your family is lucky to have you.

A great stepmom isn't perfect. She makes mistakes, but she learns from them.

A great stepmom doesn't sacrifice for others. She recognizes her own needs and limits and sets necessary boundaries.

A great stepmom doesn't always love being a stepmom. But she still shows up for herself, her partner, and her family.

A great stepmom always does her best and recognizes that her best will vary from day to day.

A great stepmom loves her partner fiercely and is focused forward to the future, not backward on the past.

IMPOSTER SYNDROME AS A STEPMOM

I first learned about imposter syndrome when I was working in Corporate America. My company's Women's Employee Resource Group brought in an author on the topic, and holy cow, it hit home. Imposter syndrome is when you feel like an imposter, or a fraud, waiting for someone to find out you aren't qualified for the position you're in.[19] So many stepmoms that I've met have experienced imposter syndrome at some point in their journeys.

Society tells us we aren't "real" moms. It feels like practically everyone has an opinion of what our roles should be, and how we should be showing up for our stepchildren. Couple all that pressure on our performance with the feelings of guilt we experience when we can't meet everyone's expectations, and it's easy for us to feel like frauds, set up to fail.

Imposter syndrome can cause you to second guess your decisions about how involved you should be with your stepchildren, what your role should be, and if you truly know what's best for your family. Instead of believing in yourself and acting with confidence, your actions are fueled by self-doubt.

At the end of this chapter, there will be additional activities to help you believe that you're not an imposter, and that you are the stepmom your family needs. Further, as you work through the remainder of the Forever Formula, you'll gain the tools and knowledge you need to build a lasting stepmom life you love. This will inevitably boost your confidence in yourself and your irreplaceable, inimitable role in your family.

TO THE STEPMOM WHO WORRIES HER FAMILY DESERVES BETTER

Stepparenting can be a beatdown. Every marriage requires hard work but add in the additional stressors that come with being in a stepfamily, and it all becomes amplified. Drama with the ex, disrespect from stepkids, a partner who parents out of guilt and acts defensive when you give feedback. ... It can be enough to reduce the strongest woman to tears and insecurities. Nearly every stepmom I know has asked herself, "Am I cut out for this? Can I really put up with all of this forever?"

We think we're the anomaly. That every other stepmom out there can tackle this role with ease and grace. We (falsely) believe we're the only ones struggling, and thus, we conclude that our partners and families deserve better or more than we can offer. To the stepmom who feels this way, please rest assured that you're not the only stepmom who has ever felt this way. But even though you aren't alone, I still don't want you to live with these feelings. The activities that follow in this chapter will help you address these feelings.

Your partner and family want you, friend. Your best is good enough, and you are adding value to your family. You are a great stepmom, and I'm here to remind you of a few important things.

YOUR PARTNER CHOOSES YOU

Every single day, your partner wakes up and chooses you. That is a big deal. Do not take that lightly. Trust is imperative for a successful relationship, and you must trust your partner when their words tell you and their actions show you, they're committed to you, and they're not searching for someone else to take your place.

You are enough. You are more than enough! If your partner wanted or needed more, they'd be pursuing another relationship, not continuing to invest in their relationship with you. You aren't a pity project or consolation prize to your partner. Reread that last sentence as many times as you need to until it really begins to sink in.

EVERY STEPMOM STRUGGLES

Stepparenting isn't an intuitive or natural role. You aren't born with, or taught growing up, how to be a successful stepmom. Most of the advice you'll receive from loved ones–or even therapists who aren't trained in stepfamily dynamics–is appropriate for nuclear families but not for a subsequent spouse in a stepfamily. Know that you will make mistakes. You will struggle. And your stepmom challenges and worries are valid.

But struggling doesn't make you a bad stepmom. You are here, seeking a better path forward; you are not a bad stepmom–far from it. Recognizing that you can't do this on your own and seeking out resources to become a happier, more peaceful, stronger stepmom proves that you're exactly where you're supposed to be. You are the stepmom your family deserves.

Struggling doesn't define you. The desire to learn how to and to put in the work necessary to become better for your partner and your family is what defines you.

YOU ADD UNIQUE VALUE TO YOUR FAMILY

I'm certain that you contribute positively to your family. You bring your own unique perspective and personality to the dynamic, and the family is more vibrant and well-rounded as a result. While it will vary by stepmom, some common themes in the value added by stepmoms I see are:

- ◆ Stability and structure
- ◆ Humor

- Feminine touch
- Unique traditions
- Focus on family time

Do any of these themes ring a bell? Or have they triggered a thought for you about the unique value that you add to your family? If you can't identify it yourself, consider asking your partner and stepchildren: "What do you like most about me? What do I contribute to our home/family?" You might be surprised by what they say! Hearing their thoughts aids in your recognition of the value you add to your family.

OVERCOMING THE DOUBTS

It can be easy to fall prey to your doubts and insecurities. I know, as I've been there. But I also know you're stronger than that. You're an incredible stepmom, and the fact you're working through these uncomfortable feelings proves my point. It's simply not enough for *me* to recognize that, however. It's critical that *you* recognize the unique value you add to your family.

You are your partner's first choice. Trust that!

Every stepmom struggles; it's not an easy role to assume. Struggling doesn't make you a bad stepmom. Trust yourself and your choices.

You do add value to your family. Trust that as well.

The upcoming activities will enable you to grow your self-worth as a stepmom. In order to become a great stepmom, you must believe that you're a great stepmom. In order to have a sustainable life of peace and happiness, you must believe that you're worthy of peace and happiness in your family. You're not an imposter; you're a critical, valuable, irreplaceable member of your family.

Activity: Create a Brag Book

You are a great stepmom, but sometimes you might just need a reminder, so set aside some time to create your brag book! A brag book is a log of memories that serves as your positive reinforcement on the hard days. Inside your brag book, place screenshot printouts of your partner's appreciation texts, add photos of your stepchild hugging you after their little league game, and journal stories that make your heart smile (like when your stepson requested that you read his bedtime story, or your stepdaughter bragged to friends that her stepmom throws the best parties). Your brag book can look like or be whatever you feel will help you get through those tough days. When you need a reminder that you're exactly where you're supposed to be, browse through your brag book. It will show you that you are making a difference, adding value to your family, and that you are important to their well-being.

Activity: Survey Your Friends and Family

In this activity, it's time to take a survey! Ask (at least) eight people who know you well to share their top three favorite qualities of yours. These could be friends, family members, in-laws, coworkers, or others in your support circle. If you feel comfortable, I encourage you to include your partner and stepchild(ren) in the people you ask.

Then, reflect upon the answers you receive.

- Are there any trends among the answers?
- Did anything surprise you?
- Which qualities do you often overlook or undervalue within yourself?
- Were there any traits mentioned that you didn't realize others saw in you?
- How did the answers make you feel?

Finally, add these answers to your brag book. It's easy to become overwhelmed with self-doubt as a stepmom, but these words are a testament to the real difference you are making in your family and the lives of others. This exercise gives you a mirror to see how your actions are actually being received and acknowledged by others. You don't have to take my word for it anymore; you'll hear it directly from those who know you best.

Activity: Write a Love Letter to Yourself

You're an incredible woman, and you deserve to revel in that knowledge a bit. In this activity, write a love letter to yourself, acknowledging how proud you are of yourself. Give yourself compliments and honor everything that you've accomplished. It's time to write down what exactly makes you so great. Don't hold back! Brag about yourself! You deserve it!

Then, on those inevitable hard days when you need a reminder of just how incredible you are, read over this love letter to yourself. Acknowledge what you've learned, how much you've grown, and what makes you special as a stepmom.

In the next chapter, I'll share the process for creating a defined stepmom role that is aligned with your values, needs, and family dynamics. We'll explore the unique factors which complicate and differentiate your role from other similar parenting roles, and by the end of the chapter, you'll have crafted an intentional, clear definition of your role. This definition will help you alleviate any guilt or outside pressure you feel to do more, be more, and to show up more. In addition, because you've learned to recognize your self-worth in this chapter, you'll now have the confidence to know this is the right role for you—and that no one else's opinion matters. It might just be my favorite thing to teach stepmoms. I love to watch the weight of expectations lifting from their shoulders. I'm excited for you to experience the same. Let's get started!

CHAPTER 5

Define an Authentic Role

As you begin to learn how to define an authentic role in your stepfamily, I want to set some expectations. I'm not about to teach you how to be a super stepmom–at least not in the traditional sense. I'm not going to encourage you to do more for your family, suppress your feelings, and let your gratitude for your partner negate your need for boundaries and self-care. You are an equal member of your family, and you need to create a stepmom role you *love*. To set expectations properly and provide you with a proven framework for defining your ideal role, you must first understand a few important facts about your roles. What stepparenting is and is *not*.

- ◆ Stepparenting is not natural.
- ◆ Stepparenting is not intuitive.
- ◆ A stepfamily is not a nuclear family.

Stepparenting is not a natural role. Nowhere else in nature do we see one maternal figure step up to help parent a child that already has involved parents. Shared parenting and stepparenting are man-made, and it can be extremely challenging learning how to navigate these unprecedented dynamics.

The real kicker is that there's immense pressure to feel and engage naturally in your family. Outsiders have opinions on what your role should be and how involved you should be in your stepchildren's lives, without ever having experienced your unique struggles. You're being judged for not loving your stepchild as your own, by people who simply don't understand. Their unrealistic expectations can lead you to experience increased guilt and exacerbated concerns and feelings of not-enoughness.

To complicate matters even more, stepparenting is not an intuitive role. The actual steps you might need to take as a stepmom (such as distancing yourself from your stepchildren, disengaging from parenting tasks, and choosing not to participate in discipline) can feel completely counterintuitive and counterproductive. But as you grow in this role, you'll learn that with stepparenting, sometimes less is actually more.

Further, stepfamilies are fundamentally different from nuclear families, and it's not a nuance that can be overlooked. The dynamics are so different that they require stepmoms to show up in a different role and serve a different purpose than parents in a nuclear family. In this section, you'll learn how they're different and what that means for your stepmom role.

A key result of a stepfamily being different from a nuclear family is that the stepmom is an outsider in the family. Maybe you've sensed this feeling before but not been able to place your finger on it. In this chapter, I'll share more about outsider feelings and the specific steps you can take to go from outsider to insider.

Once you understand and embrace these facts about your stepmom role, you're ready to dive into the rest of this chapter. Guilt is one of the most powerful–and yet, counterproductive–motivators you'll experience as you navigate stepmotherhood. Stepmoms worldwide are left feeling guilty about their emotions and reactions and the ways they show up for their stepfamilies. You'll learn how to determine if your guilt is justified and how to stop feeling guilty.

Then, you'll discover the powerful concept of relational reciprocity. Sometimes as a stepparent, you'll have to disengage from your stepchildren in order to show up best for them. It seems backward–to step back so you can step up better. And yet, somehow it works! This is one of those times where you'll definitely want to strive for balance and value quality over quantity.

Once you've rebalanced for reciprocity in your relationships, you're ready to begin defining your stepmom role. You'll explore the beliefs you're currently holding about the stepmom role, dive deep into your vision and goals for your role, and craft a two-part definition of which you can be proud. Additionally, the importance of authenticity in your stepmom role will be highlighted. When your stepmom role is aligned with your needs and values, and you can show up genuinely without fear of judgment or guilt, everything will begin to fall into place.

Defining your role is a great first step. But you must actually step into that role you've designated for yourself. Next, you'll work through the best practices for bonding with your stepchildren and disciplining them as their stepmom. You'll learn about the tools you need to strengthen those bonds and feel more confident in your new stepmom role. A defined authentic role will provide you with a framework to alleviate guilt, show up confidently day after day, and add value to your stepchildren's lives in an authentic, fulfilling way. Note, there's no one-size-fits-all approach to stepparenting. By deciding on a role that aligns with your personal values and that your family is receptive to, you'll realize that you've created the perfect role for *you* within your family. Even if it looks different than the role you or your partner expected or imagined.

A Stepfamily's Dynamics are Fundamentally Different

"If you judge a fish by its ability to climb a tree, it will live its whole life believing that it is stupid."
– Often attributed to Albert Einstein, theoretical physicist

If you're struggling to understand why your family isn't meshing, why you feel like an outsider, why you're receiving resistance from other family members, and your family just doesn't feel natural, I'm here to give you a harsh but important reality check:

A stepfamily is not a nuclear family.

Everything that we've been taught growing up, seen in popular culture, and read about in books, displays either a nuclear or a fictional blended family. Put simply, everything that we think we know about family dynamics does not apply in a real-life stepfamily.

You aren't struggling as a stepmom because you're not working hard enough, or because you're not good enough. You're struggling because stepparenting is really tough. It's a completely different animal than anything you've ever seen or experienced.

For example, I thought my experience as a child with divorced parents would give me an advantage as a stepmom. I really truly thought I knew what I was signing up for. I was so naive and blinded by love. Stepmomming required an entirely different skillset and role in my family than I ever knew existed.

Imagine that parenting your own children is like scrambling an egg, and stepparenting is like poaching an egg. There is certainly some overlap between the two: You need to know how to operate a stove and how to crack an egg. However, different tools are needed for each, and the best practices and fundamental processes are different. Having grown up your entire life eating and cooking scrambled eggs doesn't equip you to one day be able to walk into your kitchen and poach an egg to perfection.

Your knowledge of parenting roles, what you've seen in popular culture of families and ways a mom shows up in her family, and your personal experience growing up–even as a child of divorce–are not applicable experiences to joining a blended family and stepmomming to perfection.

A STEPFAMILY IS FORMED FROM LOSS

No matter how you look at it, forming a stepfamily is a result of some sort of loss. This loss can be experienced in many ways. It might be the loss of an expectation or a dream, or the tangible loss of a relationship and the nuclear family. My partner, for example, lost his marriage and his legal family unit.

Without the loss of that first relationship and family, your stepfamily wouldn't exist. Something else had to break first in order to make room for you. It's a dynamic that simply can't be ignored, as it has major impacts on a stepmom's role in a stepfamily.

IN A NUCLEAR FAMILY, EVERYONE FORMS THE CULTURE TOGETHER

In a stepfamily, the norms and habits that exist in your home between your partner and their child(ren) were developed before you joined the family.[9] As a unit, they have a certain way of doing things that they've created over time–one that feels natural and "right."

When a stepmom enters the home, she's often overwhelmed by the existing culture. She doesn't feel like she fits in, often disagreeing with some of the existing structure, rules, and norms. The home didn't need to accommodate the stepmom before, and it's very apparent. In a nuclear family, the couple developed the home's culture together. A stepmom is playing catch-up, however, and when she starts to request that the norms shift to include her, the impact is felt by everyone in the home.

IN A NUCLEAR FAMILY, EVERYONE'S POSITION IS KNOWN IN THE FAMILY

There's no question in a nuclear family who the parents are, and what their authority is. In a stepfamily, however, that position isn't as obvious. Stepchildren are often left wondering what kind of authority a new stepparent should have, especially when their other parent isn't supportive of the new stepparent's role in their lives.

Stepmoms are also left wondering what their role is exactly. Are they equal to their partner? Are they supposed to step up and be the "Mom of the Home?" Certainly, it can be challenging to figure out where you fit in, simply because it's not as obvious in a stepfamily.

IN A NUCLEAR FAMILY, PARENTS SUPPORT ONE ANOTHER

In a nuclear family, the original parents support each other and lift each other up. In a stepfamily formed by the loss of that relationship, the original parents don't always support each other. If they were amicable and agreed completely, there likely wouldn't have been a need to separate and co-parent.

In the best of cases, the parents might subtly disagree. They might have different house rules, bedtimes, and screen-time limits. While the parents may not be disparaging of each other, their differences will be noticeable. Each original parent stands on their own, without needing (or wanting) to support the other parent.

In the highest conflict scenarios, one (or both parents) is actively bad-mouthing the other to the children. There is little to no support for a relationship with or respect toward the other parent or stepparent. This vastly differs from the support you'd see in a nuclear family and requires a different approach by all involved.

SIMILARLY, IN A NUCLEAR FAMILY, PARENTS DEMAND RESPECT OF EACH OTHER

You'd be hard-pressed to find a nuclear family with parents who don't demand the respect of their co-parent. It's a parent's job to teach their child, and without respect, that's virtually impossible to do. When parents respect each other, they demand that same respect from their children. In laymen's terms, they've got each other's backs.

In terms of stepfamilies, should exes still expect and encourage their children to respect the other parent and stepparent? Of course! Do they? Not always.

A couple's separation doesn't negate the need for a parent to be respected by their children. Even if someone thinks their ex-partner isn't worthy of respect, they'd still want their children to honor that parent's wishes during their custodial time. It would be dangerous to encourage your child not to respect your co-parent, and then they subsequently disregard when their parents tell them not to touch a hot stove, right? Even when you don't love the idea of co-parenting or admire your co-parent, you still should demand respect of them.

IN A STEPFAMILY, THE CHILD PREDATES THE COUPLE[20]

Stepcouples don't get a honeymoon period to focus on each other and bask in the glow of their love before adding to their family like most original parents do. Stepcouples are immediately thrown into instant familyhood. Things become even more challenging when you factor in the fact that the parent/child relationship existed before the stepcouple's relationship. That original parent/child bond is deeper and involves more history, memories, and trust.

In this upside-down, topsy-turvy scenario, the stepcouple needs to be the family's foundation, but it's difficult to overcome the history.

IN A STEPFAMILY, THE COUPLE BOND AND PARENT–CHILD BOND IS OFTEN IN CONFLICT

Pouring time and energy into your couple bond in your stepfamily often comes at the (perceived) expense of time and energy pouring into the parent-child bond. The stepmom's partner can easily feel caught in the middle between providing for the stepmom and providing for their children. It's a delicate balance between protecting you, their partner, and making you feel welcomed and comfortable in the new family dynamic, without making their children feel replaced, demoted, or loved any less.

These two very important relationships can often feel at odds with one another, creating an unhealthy dynamic in the home, which wouldn't exist in a nuclear family.

If it hasn't become abundantly clear, nuclear families are much straightforward than stepfamilies. Their dynamics and relationships are less complicated and easier to navigate. It's why stepfamilies cannot be treated the same. A stepfamily is not a nuclear family. A stepmom is not an original parent. Your stepmom role requires something different from the role of an original parent. Let me emphasize here that this role is not less-than, not irrelevant, or not unimportant. It's simply *different.*

Activity: Journal Your Stepfamily Perspective

In this activity, it's time to grab a journal and write about how you've been treating your stepfamily like a nuclear family. Answer the following: Which differences in this chapter provided the most perspective? Where have you been spinning your wheels trying to fit a round peg into a square hole? Where do you need to pivot your perspective and approach?

Shifting from Outsider to Insider

> *"Loneliness does not come from having no people around you, but from being unable to communicate the things that seem important to you."*[21]
>
> – Carl Jung, author, psychologist, and
> founder of Analytic Psychology

Feeling left out is one of the most common struggles stepmoms face silently. Feeling all alone when you're surrounded by people you care about isn't easy to explain. You are technically part of the family, but you're not always in the innermost circle. You're included, but it can sometimes feel like just barely. You're with the people you love the most, your chosen family, and you don't always feel chosen or loved the same in return.

I've heard the act of becoming a stepmom likened to picking up a game controller and pressing play on a paused video game. Learning to adapt to norms, defining your stepmom role, determining where you fit in, and building familial relationships are just a few of the adjustments you must make to prepare for this next chapter in life. As part of this growing and blending process, you might experience feeling like an outsider in your own family.[7]

Sometimes, it's obvious that you're an outsider. Say your partner's children walk into the room and ignore you. It's clear that they only want to speak with their parent and not you. They only want to wish their parent goodnight. They intentionally bring up memories from before you entered the picture to make you feel even more excluded. In extreme instances, they might act as if you don't even exist.

Sometimes, the act of making you feel like an outsider is more subtle. It's an inside joke that you don't know about. It's the children requesting their favorite meal, a dish they know that you've never cooked before. All three of you are huddled on the couch for movie night, but they're the only ones sharing a blanket. To the naked eye, nothing is awry. However, to you, it feels obvious that you're on the outside.

And to be frank, you *are* an outsider. I say this with love (and a solution). Your partner has a relationship, history, and memories with their children that predate their relationship with you. They developed norms, inside family jokes, habits, and routines, all before you entered the picture. You find yourself on the outside because you quite literally are. This is a natural response to a very real phenomenon.

So, how do you overcome feeling like an outsider as a stepmom?

I have been in your shoes, friend. There was a time when I felt like I was an outsider in my own family–an imposter in my own home.

When they'd cuddle under that blanket while we watched a movie together, I'd feel like the odd person out.

When my stepdaughter, Krista, finished a big performance or softball game, she'd run to her mom and dad, not to me.

When my husband, Kevin, and Krista swapped stories about things that happened in the past, I was reminded that I wasn't there during that time of their lives.

No matter the ages of your stepchildren and whether or not the other parent is in the picture, the following same strategies still apply for overcoming these outsider feelings as a stepmom.

BE INTENTIONAL WITH YOUR TIME

One of the easiest ways to move past feeling like an outsider is to spend one-on-one time bonding with your stepchildren. The closer a relationship you can develop with them outside of your partner, the more comfortable things will feel in the larger family group setting.

Developing this relationship with your stepchildren will likely feel intimidating at first. I suggest you find small pockets of time where you can provide your undivided attention to your stepchild(ren) and focus on getting to know them better and enabling them to get to know you better. Any small amount of time is a win—even 15–20 minutes here and there can make a massive difference. This relationship needs to develop naturally, and small pockets of time are easier to manage for both you and your stepchildren. Those small moments do add up, and eventually, you'll find that you both feel more comfortable with each other. As a result, you'll begin to feel more like a part of the family and less like an outsider when the entire family is together. You'll now have bonds, inside jokes, and memories tying you to your stepchildren too, not just to your partner.

Additionally, ensure that as a stepmom you designate time to spend intentionally together. Quality time as a family creates shared memories and cultivates a safer space for everyone to feel included. As a family, explore new activities together, institute family movie nights where you alternate who gets to pick the flick, or brainstorm together to create a different tradition. Instead of continuing to do things that leave you outside looking in on their fun, try new experiences with them. Being in a new environment together gives you equal footing and shared experiences in which to grow.

What are some low-pressure activities you'd enjoy doing with your stepchild? (Putting together a puzzle, going for ice cream).

What are some activities that your stepchild enjoys doing? How could you meet them where they're at? (Sending TikTok videos of cats doing silly things, watching them play video games, offering to drop them off at work).

What are some activities you enjoyed when you were your stepchild's age? How could you share those with them? (Ice skating, reading *Harry Potter* or *The Boxcar Children*).

Now, circle or highlight one activity from each list you'd like to try first. Choose one and schedule it during your next custodial time!

Keep this list handy for future visitations to further enhance your relationship with your stepchild.

DISCUSS YOUR CONCERNS WITH YOUR PARTNER

If you find yourself consistently feeling like an outsider in your stepfamily and your partner is inadvertently contributing to those feelings, explain to them what they're doing and how it makes you feel. Your partner will likely never understand your perspective. There's a good chance your partner doesn't see the things that are making you feel left out. It's an unintentional act, but by speaking to them about it, you give them the opportunity to become aware and correct it. Cluing your partner into the ways they might be exacerbating your outsider feelings is the first step in helping you eliminate (or reduce) some of the isolating behavior.

FEEL FREE TO EXCUSE YOURSELF FROM AWKWARD MOMENTS

If you're caught in a moment where you're feeling left out, you're allowed to excuse yourself. Give your partner and their children the space needed to be comfortable in their bond and memories without sacrificing your own peace of mind. You don't have to continue being uncomfortable just to make others feel more comfortable.

I don't advise making a big deal about your departure, but rest assured that you're always entitled to remove yourself from situations costing you your peace. Try something quick like, "I'm going to go check the laundry" or "I'll be back in a bit." Note, if you don't speak up, they might worry they've upset you or wonder where you've gone, calling far more attention to the moment than is necessary. By speaking up, you've avoided that awkward moment altogether.

If you are experiencing outsider feelings, please know that so many other stepmoms are experiencing these same feelings. You are not alone in this journey. What you are experiencing right now is only temporary. Start taking baby steps toward becoming an insider, and with enough time, you'll begin to notice a shift.

Activity: Create a Plan to Shift from Outsider to Insider

In this activity, grab a piece of paper and write down your thoughts for each of these statements:

1. Brainstorm times when you've felt like an outsider in the last two to four weeks. Leave space for a response after each of those items you've written down.
2. Going line by line, write underneath each scenario what you would've needed to feel like an insider (or not like an outsider) in each one.
3. Then, highlight (or circle) the person you feel responsible for each solution.
4. Next, create a new list of ways that your partner could've helped you feel less like an outsider and more like an insider.
5. Discuss these scenarios and strategies with your partner.
6. Finally, create an exit plan to keep in your back pocket for those awkward moments, just in case.

Understanding and Resolving Guilt

"Guilt, shame, and criticism are some of the most damaging forces in your life."[18]

– Jen Sincero, author of *You Are a Badass*

Guilt is practically useless. It rarely serves a positive purpose in life. Consider the last time you did something after thinking to yourself, "I should do this, or I'll feel guilty." How did you feel afterward? Did you feel energized and better aligned with your role and family? Or did you feel burned out, frustrated, or resentful?

Guilt often arises from the false belief that you "should" be doing something, even when your intuition suggests otherwise. Continuously making decisions out of guilt–or trying to avoid feeling guilty–can quickly lead to resentment and unhappiness. When you don't honor your own values and needs, you create conflict within yourself.

Stop Shoulding on Yourself

> *"Stop shoulding on yourself."*
> – Often attributed to Albert Ellis, American psychologist

So much of a stepmom's guilt originates from those "shoulds": How she should show up in the family, how she should feel about her stepchildren, how she should (or shouldn't) set boundaries. All a stepmom needs do is follow her hierarchy of priorities: self, relationship, family.

Remember: These are your partner's children, not yours. It means most of the burden of parenting should land on their shoulders, not yours.

I used to wake up early every day to see my stepdaughter off to school alongside my husband. I thought I would feel guilty for not seeing her until she got home from school, so I stayed up late working and got up early with them. As you can probably imagine that combination didn't result in a delightful Mary Poppins of a stepmom. Instead, I was a sleepy, irritable stepmom most days.

When my stepdaughter didn't want to eat breakfast, I quickly became frustrated. If we were running behind, I would become easily stressed. Acting out of guilt and waking up early with the family when I truly needed more sleep to be a great stepmom did not help any of us. In fact, it led to even more conflict for our family. Remember when I said stepparenting can be counterintuitive? Case in point.

The Four Types of People Who Say "Yes" When They Want to Say "No"

Many stepmoms feel guilty for saying "no." They think that because they technically could do something, they are required then to do it. (Spoiler alert: You aren't.) In her book, *F*ck No!*, New York Times bestselling author Sarah Knight, details four different types of people who say "yes" when they really want to say "no."[22] First, consider each of these four types, and then decide which, if any, resonate with you.

THE PEOPLE PLEASER

Many women are socialized to be people pleasers–people who feel the need to constantly please others. We are taught not to take up too much space–quite literally but also emotionally and figuratively. Many of us are raised to place the needs of all others before our own.

People pleasers say "yes" when they want to say "no" because:

◆ They don't want to disappoint someone.
◆ They feel like they have an obligation to others.
◆ They don't want to appear rude, or
◆ They want others to like them.

If you place others' needs before your own, avoid sharing your feelings if it contradicts your family's, or say "I'm fine" when you're actually not, you might be a people pleaser.

In 1942, Joan Crawford is attributed with saying, "You are not required to set yourself on fire to keep other people warm." Let that sink in. How might you be setting yourself on fire to keep those around you warm?

THE OVERACHIEVER

Many of the stepmoms I've coached have been overachievers. They don't just want to be OK stepmoms. They want to be The Best Stepmom. They are determined to master the art of stepmomming and to add immense value to the lives of their partner and stepchildren.

Overachievers say "yes" when they want to say "no" because:

◆ They want everything to be perfect.
◆ They never want to give an impression of laziness or apathy.
◆ They have a competitive spirit and want to outdo themselves or the other parent.
◆ They believe they'll do a task better than anyone else.

If you take on too much in your stepfamily out of a desire to prove your worth, or because you believe you know best, you might be an overachiever.

THE FOMO'ER

FOMO is the Fear of Missing Out. I've met many stepmoms who will commit to attending all the little league games and accompanying their partner to every pickup and dropoff because they have a fear of missing out. They don't want to miss out on their stepchildren's lives, their partner's experience with the other parent, or any potentially meaningful or fun family moments. They are FOMO'ers.

FOMO'ers say "yes" when they want to say "no" because:

♦ Regret fuels their decisions.
♦ They don't want to miss out on potentially fun or rewarding experiences.
♦ While they might not enjoy being overwhelmed by taking on too much, they fear the consequences of not joining.

If you say "yes" when everything in your body is screaming "no" because you're worried about being left out of something, you're a FOMO'er, my friend.

THE PUSHOVER

A pushover values harmony over everything else. They will avoid conflict over self-preservation every single time. I've met some pushover stepmoms, but often, due to the perspective that we discussed in Chapter 1, I've met a lot more pushover *partners* of stepmoms.

Pushovers say "yes" when they want to say "no" because:

♦ They hate confrontation.
♦ They take the path of least resistance.
♦ They don't have much willpower.

If you know you really should say "no" but don't because you're worried it could disrupt the peace or upset your partner or stepchildren, you're probably a pushover.

Do any of these four types of people sound like you? Or like your partner? How might these behaviors be preventing you from showing up as the stepmom you want to be? How can recognizing this pattern help you to start saying "no" more confidently and more often? Take some time to consider what you need from your partner to overcome these fears and recognize that you can best serve your family with a "no" sometimes, guilt-free.

ASSUAGING GUILT

Knight encourages us to say "no" to things we can't, shouldn't, and don't want to do.[23] I believe every stepmom needs this reminder.

For example, let's pretend your stepson has a hockey game tonight. You're wondering if you should go or not. Realize that you're allowed to say "no" if:

- You *can't* attend due to a conflicting work event.
- You *shouldn't* attend because you'll see their other parent and there will be conflict.
- You *don't want to* attend because it's been a long day, and you really would love to take a bubble bath, relax, and listen to your favorite music in an empty house.

Even if you're worried that you'll feel guilty for not attending, check your motivation. Are you attending because you want to support your stepson and are excited to watch him play? If so, go to the game! Or are you attending out of guilt, or to avoid feeling guilty? If that's your motivation, it's better to take a pass.

Knight teaches us, "Guilt is the most powerful and the most counterproductive motivator for doing things we can't, shouldn't, and don't want to do."[24] The key is to investigate why you're feeling guilty before you allow that guilt to drive you toward saying "yes" when you want to say "no."

To do this, Knight recommends asking yourself these four questions:

- "Is your guilt warranted (because you're doing something objectively wrong)?
- Or is it unwarranted (because you've done nothing wrong)?
- Is it purely self-imposed (nobody has said anything, but you still feel guilty)?
- Or is it the result of outside pressure (other people have an opinion on how you should show up as a stepmom)?"[25]

Once you identify the cause (warranted or unwarranted) and the guilt source (yourself or others), you can proceed accordingly to assuage your guilt. To be clear, examples of objectively wrong are being neglectful, abusive, or breaking the law. Not attending your stepson's hockey game because you need a breather, not making dinner for an ungrateful child, and refusing to do laundry for your stepchildren are *not* examples of actions that are objectively wrong.

Scenario 1: You're actually guilty of doing something objectively wrong, and it doesn't matter if it's self-imposed or the result of outside pressure. An example would be totally ignoring and/or being mean to your stepchildren. If you want to stop feeling guilty, then stop doing it.

Scenario 2: You are not doing something wrong, and someone else is putting pressure on you to feel guilty. An example of this would be defining a disengaged role that feels aligned to you, and your mother-in-law is trying to tell you that it's wrong and you need to be more engaged. You know the role that is best for you in the family, and no one else gets an opinion about it. You're not doing anything wrong.

First, I want you to think: Has the other person verbalized these comments? Or is it possible you're reading into their actions and making assumptions? We often totally misjudge how interested in our lives other people actually are. It's a humbling reality.

If they have directly verbalized these judgmental remarks, it doesn't change the fact that you have done nothing for which to feel guilty. It's likely this person is projecting their own insecurities onto you, because they don't think they're allowed to say "no" or set boundaries of their own. Hold firm in the knowledge that you haven't done anything objectively wrong. You are entitled to your boundaries and to set the role that is best aligned with your values and your family's needs.

Scenario 3: You're not doing something wrong, and you're placing pressure on yourself. Unfortunately, I see this all too often. Stepmoms hold themselves to such ridiculously high standards, and when they can't live up to them, they feel guilty. If this is what you're experiencing, you need to give yourself permission to set boundaries to protect your peace. When you do, you'll become a better stepmom. Use Table 5.1 to help you begin reframing your guilty thoughts. You deserve freedom from unnecessary guilt and pressure.

Table 5.1   Reframing Guilty Thoughts

Original Guilty Thought	Reframed Thought
"I don't want to go to this event without my stepkids."	"My stepkids' lives don't end when they're in their other home, and ours shouldn't either."
"I don't want to attend this event with my friends/family solo when my stepkids are home."	"The best way I can show up for my family and marriage is by doing things that recharge my battery. Plus, it's important for my stepchildren to get time with their parent without me."
"I look forward to my stepkids leaving and going to their other home."	"Alone time with my partner is crucial for growing and maintaining a successful relationship."
"I should really go to my stepson's soccer game today, even though I really don't want to."	"I'm allowed to say 'no' and should say 'no' when my intuition tells me to. Not attending is the best thing I can do for my relationship. I am still a good stepmom."

As you continue to develop a strong, defined role, you'll become more confident, alleviating guilty feelings.

Activity: Just Say "No"

As a stepmom, you're bound to have a full life with everything you, your spouse, and their kids have going on in life. Surely, there's something that is scheduled in which you really don't want to take part. It's now time to exercise your power to answer "No, thank you."

Today, say "no" to something you can't, shouldn't, or don't want to do in your stepfamily. Then, journal about the experience. How did it feel to say "no?" Was it hard? Empowering? Did you feel guilt, relief, or something else? Consider how you would have felt if you'd said "yes" instead. Are you grateful you didn't? What would it take for you to feel more confident saying "no" in the future?

Relational Reciprocity and Stepping Back

"Your value is not dependent on your sacrifice."

– Amelia Nagoski, DMA

If you've ever felt underappreciated as a stepmom or thought to yourself, "I have done so much for all of you, why can't I just get [respect, love, appreciation, acknowledgment, and so on] in return?" then this part of the chapter is for you, my friend. Here, I'm going to help you unpack this very important topic so that you can understand why you feel underappreciated and teach you how to stop letting it grow into resentment.

One key principle in stepfamily relationships is reciprocity, meaning you should be receiving as much as you are giving to your partner, their children, their ex-partner, and so on. If the effort you put into these relationships isn't reciprocated, you will overextend yourself, become burned out, and feel taken for granted. Resentment will begin growing in its place.

Say you spend time making your stepdaughter's lunch, and she complains about it when she comes home from school. You invested time making a thoughtful grocery list to include her favorites, shopping, prepping, and packing her lunch. (Not to mention the financial investment, but I digress.) You put a lot of effort into her lunch to give her a reason to smile in the middle of the school day. Then she returns, complaining that she didn't get the snack she wanted, the sandwich tasted like crap, and you forgot her dessert. Or maybe she's simply apathetic, remarking, "Meh, it was fine." Her response does not match your effort at all. You're at level ten, she is at a level one.

This imbalance, as depicted in Figure 5.1, causes tension in stepfamily relationships. You will either feel frustrated with your stepdaughter–or worse, with your partner. Instead of expecting more from your stepdaughter (even if it is totally reasonable to expect her to appreciate you making her lunch), match her effort level. Bring yourself down to a level one too. Grab the Lunchables kit at the store, load the school lunch account with money, or pack up and send dinner leftovers to school. Do not put in extra effort if it isn't being reciprocated. To put it simply, meet her on whatever level she's at.

Usually, I receive a lot of pushback on this idea when I first present it to stepmoms. It simply goes against everything that we have been taught about motherhood. We are told to be selfless, sacrificial, and give to others before we give to ourselves. If that's sustainable to

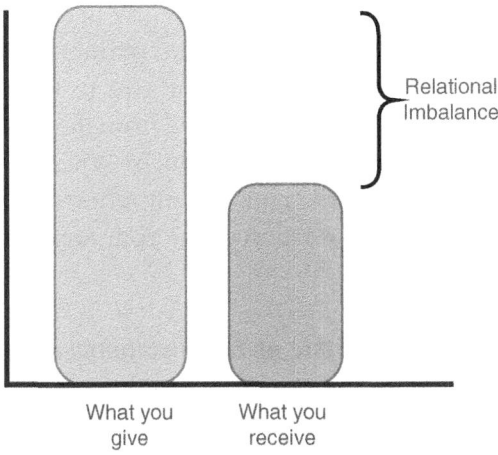

Figure 5.1   Relational imbalance portrayal.

you as a mom, brilliant. I love that for you! But I assure you it isn't sustainable as a stepmom. There isn't a natural love to offset the sacrifice and level-set the resentment. Stepmotherhood doesn't offer the same natural fulfillment that original motherhood does. Your stepchildren aren't owed your energy, and you aren't owed theirs. As a result, you must match their energies.

The one exception to this rule is if you can do something without expectation. If you love helping with homework–maybe education is a primary core value of yours–and how your stepchild responds to your assistance does not affect you, then do it. Help with math homework, get them prepped for a social studies quiz, or assist with that science project. But the moment that you become frustrated they're not paying attention, appreciating you, or respecting the time and energy you're providing, you must step away! Even if only for a little bit.

Stepfamily relationships are precarious, and the stepmom-stepchild relationship is the most precarious of all. If you are feeling an imbalance in what you are giving and what you are receiving in return, reset your role to meet your stepchild on their level. Stop pouring energy into tasks that aren't being reciprocated. Step away from anything extra you're giving if it's tied to an expectation of a relationship, respect, or appreciation in return. Ensuring relational reciprocity is the best thing you can do for that relationship. When you aren't burned out, resentful, overextended, and feeling unappreciated, you show up as a more grateful, present woman, partner, and stepmom.

Take some time to reflect on what you give to the relationship with your stepchildren and what you receive from them. Ask yourself these questions: Where am I giving too much? Where are my step-children not appreciating or recognizing my efforts? Where might an imbalance be affecting my relationships? Your answers just might surprise you.

Activity: Evaluate the Current State of Your Relational Reciprocity

1. On a blank sheet of paper, draw a line down the center from top to bottom.
2. On the left side of the paper, write the header, "What I give." On the right side, write the header, "What I receive."
3. Then, list out what you're doing for your stepchild on the left side, and what you're receiving from them (both positive and negative) on the right side.
4. Finally, reflect on the two columns. Do you have reciprocity? If not, where might you need to disengage?

WHAT IS (AND IS NOT) DISENGAGING

Perhaps you've heard of the terms disengaging or stepping back before. In stepmom circles, this tool has a variety of names, but for the purpose of this section, I'll use the terms interchangeably. When I first heard about disengaging from your stepchildren, I was completely taken aback. It felt counterintuitive at best and cruel at worst. After all, isn't a stepmom supposed to play an active role in her stepchildren's lives and do so with a smile on her face? At least that's what we've been told to do.

As a child of divorce myself, I had a hard time wrapping my brain around why a stepmom would need to disengage. Though an incorrect assumption, I thought stepping back from stepchildren was done with malice and intended to create a divide. In reality, it's a means to show up as your best self in hopes of further connecting with the family. It's about defining a role that enables you to have the best chance of a positive relationship with your stepchild. If you're feeling burned out or unappreciated, or recognize a lack of reciprocity in your relationships, it might be time to step back from them.

Disengaging is widely misinterpreted and misunderstood, and it gets a bad rap. I'm here to dispel some of those myths. By stepping back, you're taking a critical step in defining your true and authentic role in your family, enabling you to live with sustainable peace and happiness in your stepfamily. If you want to find lasting joy and a relationship that beats the odds, you must find that perfect role for you.

Disengaging isn't neglecting or being abusive to your stepchildren. To be clear, taking a step back in your stepmom role does not mean you're allowing your stepchildren to become neglected. You will ensure that they're still cared for, having all their needs met, and so on. Now, you don't have permission to be mean or disrespectful to your stepchildren. Even when you've chosen to disengage, you should still treat them with kindness when you are present. You continue to say "hello," you smile at them, and you give off a welcoming aura.

Disengaging from your stepchildren isn't "checking out" of your family or romantic relationship. Disengaging in your stepmom role solely improves your relationships. It helps you to refocus on and reprioritize your values and goals. It's not a way of giving up or checking out. When done correctly, taking a step back gives you renewed energy and reprioritized contributions to make in your family. This process enables you to later step up and step into your family, in the most impactful and beneficial way possible for them. For example, because I took a step back from morning routines with my stepdaughter, I was more present when she got home from school. I could prepare a snack for her and have a healthier, happier mood when she walked in the door, than I would have had when I suffered through challenging mornings.

Disengaging doesn't mean that you've given up on your family or that you're a bad stepmom. The best stepmoms know how to evaluate what's not working and to pivot when necessary. Recognizing that a certain type of engagement isn't serving your relationship with your stepchild or your stepfamily, is definitely a skill. We step back because we care, not because we've given up. My client, Clarissa, stopped accompanying her partner to custodial pickups after recognizing how draining they were on her energy and mood. She would become triggered by the other parent's disrespect toward Clarissa's partner, and it would leave her feeling agitated, frustrated, and frankly, angry. She wasn't as excited to see her stepchildren as a result, and the ride home was fraught with tension. By stepping back from pick-ups, Clarissa removed the trigger and was better able to welcome her stepchildren home with a genuine smile and positive attitude. The extra 20 minutes that she spent in the car with them wasn't beneficial to anyone, so she took a step back to step up into being an even better stepmom.

You're Allowed to Change Your Mind

You might be thinking, "But Kristen, I've already been so involved for so long. I can't step back now! What kind of message would that send?" I hear you. I do. And you are allowed to change your mind. If the role you're currently taking on doesn't serve you, then you cannot continue in that same role. Something must indeed change.

Our role as a stepmom is fluid and requires flexibility and adaptability. It's okay to change your mind as your stressors, needs, and relationships evolve. Just because something (e.g., being involved with bedtime) is what you wanted or needed before, doesn't mean that it's what you want or need today. It's okay to need or want something different as you and/or your stepchildren change. In my early days as a stepmom, I wanted to be an equal in all ways to my partner. Notably, I wanted to be involved in rules enforcement and discipline. Today, I have a much more hands-off approach with discipline. I support Kevin in correcting my stepdaughter's behavior and assigning consequences. I changed my mind on wanting to be involved with discipline because it was no longer aiding in me being the best stepmom I could be—for myself, my husband, or my stepdaughter.

You don't need to disengage from your family forever! It can be a temporary fix as you repair relational reciprocity and redefine your role.

HOW TO DISENGAGE FROM YOUR STEPCHILDREN

In some rare and extreme cases, stepmoms need to fully disengage for a period of time, then begin reengaging slowly with safer, simpler tasks. But often, stepmoms simply need to reevaluate where they can be involved peacefully, and where their efforts might be contributing to an imbalance.

I think about my client, Allison, who had been a stepmom for 11.5 years before joining my small group coaching program. Her partner worked long hours, and she took on virtually all the childrearing of her full-time stepchildren. She came to me burned out, resentful, and struggling to see a way forward, with fractured relationships with her stepchildren and partner. Because Allison was at a breaking point after over a decade of overextending herself without reciprocity, it was important that she take the world's biggest step back from all things stepparenting. She would no longer drive her stepdaughter to school. She stopped making dinner. She gave herself the space and grace to navigate a new normal with a better-defined role that would benefit her entire family.

If things aren't as extreme for you as they were for Allison, evaluate where you believe your efforts aren't being reciprocated. What tasks do you dread? What robs you of your peace? Some of the most common answers I hear to these questions are: Custody exchanges, cooking dinner (because your stepchildren don't like or appreciate your cooking), homework help, and disciplinary feedback. Your answers to these questions will help you recognize where you need to step back.

COMMUNICATING YOUR DECISION TO YOUR PARTNER

Once you've decided where you need to step back, communicate this decision to your partner. Not for their permission, but so they can support you when you do and pick up any slack.

This isn't a decision that you made lightly or selfishly. It's a decision you made for the health and happiness of your entire family. You need to stand firm in that decision. When you aren't resentful or burned out, you will show up better for your family. You will enjoy them more, and they will enjoy you more! It's a win-win for everyone when a stepmom sets the role that feels authentically right for her and enables her to thrive and truly come alive in her stepfamily.

Proper communication in this scenario is vital. Let your partner know this disengaging isn't an attack on them or their children, a strike from parenting duties until some demands are met, or any other sort of negative action. Disengaging from your stepchildren will actually enable you to be the best you for your family.

Be patient. Remember that disengaging likely seemed harsh or felt uncomfortable to you when you first heard of it. Allow your partner time to adjust to the idea and recognize the merits of your decision.

In the end, however, if your partner doesn't support your decision, that doesn't mean you shouldn't move forward with your resolution to step back. Would I love it if you had your partner's support? Of course. Is it necessary? No. Your partner has no right to expect more from you than they are willing to give themselves. Furthermore, your boundaries do not require permission or approval. You've made the decision you believe is best for your family, and that is imperative for a sustainable stepmom life of peace.

Think about the tasks that you're giving up. Are they absolutely necessary, or just nice to do? If they're definitely necessary, and your partner is unwilling or unable to step up to fill the void, hire it out. Do not sacrifice your own needs for someone else's. You've come this far; don't give up because of a bump in the road.

Let's look at a couple of examples:

Remember Allison? When she took her giant step back, her stepdaughter no longer had a ride to the mall with her friends. Was this Allison's responsibility? No. Her stepdaughter asked a friend for a ride if she really wanted to go. Going shopping with friends isn't a critical task; Allison didn't need to spend time finding a substitute driver. She then could focus on reclaiming her peace instead, which would eventually allow her to step back into tasks she could enjoy.

Another client's stepdaughter absolutely hated doing her homework. She would get distracted, do everything she could to procrastinate, and the process literally took hours each and every night. My client became so frustrated with her stepdaughter when they worked on her homework together, that she decided it was something from which she needed to step back. In this scenario, homework is a necessary task. Her stepdaughter did need help working on her assignments for school. Dad worked late and couldn't help with homework, so they signed her up with the local tutoring center. Her stepdaughter received the help she needed, and stepmom protected her peace and her relationship with her stepdaughter. It was a win-win!

Once you've stepped back from tasks that cost you your peace, you're able to focus on the ways you can interact meaningfully and with the most impact. As those relationships progress, you can reengage with tasks that feel in tune with your intuition again. Our roles are ever evolving, and you're in control. Choose the role today that feels reciprocal, fulfilling, and aligned with your core values. Choose the role that makes you the partner and stepmom you desire to be, within those conditions. In the next section, you'll explore the beliefs and goals of your role and then work on your first clear definition of your role.

Beliefs and Defining Your Role

"Today you are You, that is truer than true. There is no one alive who is Youer than You."[26]

– Dr. Seuss, children's author and illustrator

This might be the most important lesson of this entire book. At the very least, it's the one I most needed to read when I first became a stepmom. Everyone has an opinion on what your stepmom role should look like. Your mother-in-law wants you to love your stepchild as your own. Your partner expects you to fill a similar role in the house that their ex did. Society expects you to give sacrificially, but they also see you as less than an original parent. It can be hard to tune out all the noise.

It's easy to fall victim to the "shoulds" and sacrificing for others. So many stepmoms let their own needs take a backseat to their partner's and stepchildren's needs. While noble, this practice isn't sustainable long term. Further, the "shoulds" they hear or think about their role motivate them to show up differently than their intuition is telling them would be best and most aligned with their capacity and needs. When others tell you that you "should" love your stepchildren as your own, but you don't, you either spiral and retreat, or dive headfirst into the role and do as much as you can in order to force those feelings to happen. Unfortunately, neither of those is going to achieve your goal of loving them more naturally, helping you feel better or have lasting peace.

To help tune out the "shoulds" and recognize the stepmom role that's best for you, we're going to explore your beliefs about and desires for your stepmom role. The answers to these questions will directly translate into your definition of your stepmom role. I know how tempting it can be to skip over the journal prompts when you're reading a book. I implore you to resist the temptation. Get out a pen and paper or open your computer's word processor and really dive into each of these questions. Trust this process. It has worked for the hundreds of stepmoms I've worked with before you, and I know it will work for you too.

After you have crafted your definition of your ideal stepmom role, I'll explore the value of authenticity in your stepfamily relationships. Enabling yourself to show up authentically in your family will bring you newfound peace and confidence. I'm giving you permission to show up as the stepmom you are, not the stepmom you think you need to be. You'll begin to experience a life-changing shift as you embrace this new role.

As I've mentioned, the stepmom role is fluid. What your stepchildren need from you will look different in each stage of life. When your stepdaughter is feeling especially close to her mom as a teenager, she might pull away from you a bit. When your stepson begins middle school and high school, he may stop asking for family movie night and stepmom/stepson one-on-one time. How much you can give in your relationships is directly tied to how much you receive in return, so your role will naturally fluctuate.

YOUR STEPPARENTING BELIEFS

The beliefs you carry may subconsciously influence how present and engaged you are in your family. You might be pushing yourself too hard to show up how you think you "should." Or you might be retreating because you believe that's your place.

Activity: Explore Your Stepparenting Beliefs

Journal your answers to the following questions as you explore your stepparenting beliefs. Note, there are no wrong answers as you explore your beliefs and desires in these journal prompts, only honest ones. Do your best not to censor your thoughts or write what you think your answer "should" be.

1. What things should a stepmom do in her family?
2. Do you expect your stepchildren to love you? If so, is it the same love they share with their parents, or a different type of love?
3. Do you expect to love your stepchildren? If so, what kind of love is it?
4. Do you want the kids think of you as another "mom," an important adult figure, a friend, or something else?
5. In what ways do you hope to contribute to your step-child's life?
6. How does society view stepmoms? How does this affect your perspective?
7. When your stepchildren are grown and look back on their childhood, what do you hope they say about you? How would you like them to remember their experience of you?
8. What does it mean about you if you struggle in your role?
9. What was your childhood experience with stepparents? How does that influence how you show up in your stepfamily?
10. Which activities do you enjoy doing with your stepchildren?
11. Which activities do you not enjoy doing with your stepchildren?
12. What are your strengths? How do they benefit your stepchildren?
13. What are your partner's strengths? What makes them a great parent?
14. How can you best support your partner's parenting strengths?

When you think you're ready, move on to the next section to consolidate these answers into a concise definition of your role.

DEFINING YOUR ROLE

I hope this soul-searching journaling gave you some clarity on where your roadblocks originate from and enabled you to hone in on what is important to you. I love this exercise because it helps to filter out some of the noise that gets in the way of how you show up as a stepmom. I also think it really helps to refocus you on what matters, like your impact. It's easy to get distracted by the daily minutiae and lose sight of the larger impact you want to make on your family.

To define your role, think about how you might fill in the blanks of these two sentences:

My role as a stepmom is to: _____.

I show this by: _____.

It might take a few iterations before you find the perfect wording, but practice makes perfect! The first part is essentially a purpose or vision statement. Describe the conceptual impact you want to make as a stepmom. The second half of your definition requires drilling down farther. How will you tangibly make this impact? For my corporate ladies, if the first part is your vision, the second part is your key performance indicators (KPIs). The vision gives you a way to easily keep your eye on the prize. And the KPIs empower you with a path to reach your target. They'll hold you accountable and keep you on track.

Here are my answers for this exercise:

My role as a stepmom is to:

◆ Love my husband, Kevin, well.
◆ Role model healthy behaviors and values.
◆ Be a safe space for my stepdaughter, Krista.

I show this by:

◆ Speaking Kevin's love language regularly.
◆ Prioritizing my marriage.
◆ Having regular check-ins with Krista and reminding her I'm here to talk if she needs anything.
◆ Always acting as if I have little eyes on me.
◆ Owning my mistakes.

You'll notice that I found it easier to define my role using bullet points. There's no single correct way to define your role, so use a structure which works best for you. Before crafting your working-role definition, proceed to the next section on authenticity. It's imperative that your role be one you can comfortably show up in genuinely. For the longest time, this was a missing piece for me.

AUTHENTICITY

In my early days as a stepmom, I tried so hard to be version 2.0 of Kevin's ex. For example, I worked diligently to show up for my partner and his daughter in the same ways his ex had (e.g., cooking dinner, keeping a clean home, doing arts and crafts together). But it felt forced. It felt like I was going through the motions and failing to do any of those things perfectly. It left me stressed out and further than ever from the life of peace of which I dreamed.

Burned out, I was growing more and more resentful as the days passed. I wondered, could I do this? Was I cut out for the stepmom role? Does my family deserve someone better than me? I felt like I was failing because I was trying to show up in my family in a way that wasn't authentic to me. I wasn't being true to myself, my strengths, and the tasks I wanted to do in and for my family.

Krista's mom is a trained, incredibly talented artist. She creates the most beautiful art. Trying to replicate this role in my home for my stepdaughter simply wasn't possible. I can draw a cute stick figure, but that's about it. My family didn't need me to be "Mom of my house" (and neither does yours!). They needed me to show up as myself, showcasing my strengths and the unique value I can add to my stepdaughter's life.

She didn't need me to cook as well as her mom or to create art with her. She does that with her mom. She needed me to sing and dance badly in the kitchen while I likely burned dinner, introduce her to *The Boxcar Children* and other favorite book series, and be the empathetic ear of a fellow stepchild. She needed to see and learn from the true, authentic me. The day that I realized it and started showing up as me, everything changed. My "light" came back, and our family dynamics shifted.

When I think about showing up authentically as a stepmom, I think of my client, Jessica. She was a driven, successful realtor before meeting her dream man and his children from a prior marriage. When Jessica became a stepmom, she put her all into the role, channeling all of her time, energy, and love into being the best stepmom she could possibly be. But when she came to me burned out and discouraged, I challenged Jessica on her core values and true behaviors she wanted to role model for her new family. She realized that the successful careerwoman she'd been before becoming a stepmom had started to slip away a bit. Her stepchildren needed to see her taking the calls, writing the contracts, and hosting the open houses. The more she allowed herself to relax and show up authentically in her family, not just the way she thought she needed to show up, the more genuinely everyone connected. She even took her stepson to an open house with her, and he marveled at how good at her job she is!

Identify the ways that *you* add something special to your family and the tasks that you enjoy doing for your family. In truth, the day I realized that my inability to show up authentically for my family was actually doing a disservice to my family, I began showing up as *me* instead of who I thought I was supposed to be, and everything changed. I was my true self again, and our family dynamics shifted for the better.

Bring your "light" back, stepmom. Show up in the role that feels right for you and get back to enjoying your family and home.

Activity: Craft Your Role Definition

Define your role using the two-part framework just discussed. Consider what value you want to add, and how you can show up authentically in your family.

My role as a stepmom is to: _____.

I show this by: _____.

Bonding with Your Stepchildren and Discipline

"The quality of your relationships determines the quality of your life."[27]

– Esther Perel, relationship expert and psychotherapist

Writing this part of the book feels like a lot of pressure! There are so many factors that contribute to the stepparent-stepchild relationship, and I want you to have the strongest bond possible. The very first thing you need to do is check all your expectations at the door. The relationship you should have with your stepchild is the one that works best for the two of you within your family dynamics. Not the one either of their original parents wants you to have, or your sister-in-law, or the one you see that influencer having on Instagram with their stepchild. Give yourself the freedom to build the bond that works best for *you*.

HOW TO SPEND TIME IN A STEPFAMILY

In this section, let's explore the best ways to spend time as a stepfamily. Four distinct time blocks should be happening regularly: Original Parent-Child, Stepmom-Child, Stepmom-Partner, and Family Time. If any of the time blocks feel daunting, know that I'll equip you with proven strategies to enhance your relationships.

Original Parent-Child

One-on-one time between your partner and their child is proven to have several benefits. I would argue it's not optional; it's imperative. Here are just a few of the benefits:

- It shows the child that they're not losing their parent and that not everything is changing.
- It gives them unencumbered time to strengthen their bond.
- It allows the stepmom time to herself. She can use this time to relax and recharge for more family time.

A parent recoupling is terrifying for children. When they are reassured that their time with their parent won't be compromised, it eases that transition for them.

When my dad met my stepmom, I felt so intimidated. I thought he would care more about her than me. I thought love, affection, and quality time were a zero-sum game, that loving and spending time with his new wife meant he would no longer love or spend time with me. I needed the reassurance that I wasn't going to lose him–that our relationship wasn't going to change as a result of his marriage.

Stepmom–Child

One-on-one time for stepmoms with their stepchildren can solve a lot of problems.

Want them to respect your authority? Spend more time with them and earn their respect.

Want to feel less like an outsider in your home? Spend more time with them and develop a relationship that feels more natural and less forced.

Want to give your partner time for self-care so they can show up as their best self for you? You guessed it: Spend one-on-one time with your stepchild.

Want to resolve resentment toward your stepchild? Creating new positive associations will help offset the negative ones.

I'll discuss more of the "how" in a minute, but for now, start wrapping your brain around the idea of additional one-on-one time with your stepchild.

Stepmom–Partner

It may seem obvious, but I'm going to call it out anyway. You need to spend time as a couple separate from the children. Yes, even during your custodial time.

Go for a walk together every morning. Set a standing lunch date on Thursdays. Set a bedtime for the kids on weekends: "You don't have to go to sleep, but you do need to be in your rooms by 9 p.m.! It's adult swim!"

Your relationship needs nurturing. You two need connection. You show up better for the entire family when you show up for each other in your relationship.

Family Time

Again, this may seem obvious, but it's crucial to have family time together. This time together enables you to deepen bonds, create a new inclusive culture, and enables everyone to feel safer amid the changing dynamics.

Try to choose activities that are low pressure and high fun. I love a good family game night or a trip to the local water park. Make memories and have fun–that's the goal.

Family Fun Activities (FFA)

I first heard about the FFA from a local therapist for adolescents, Sharon Scott. The premise is simple. You designate a recurring family playdate, and for each instance, the person who decides the activity rotates.[28] Everyone else puts on a smile and is present for their family member's activity choice–even if it's not their preferred activity.

The only two rules: It can't take very long, and it can't be too expensive. So, my stepdaughter, Krista, couldn't decide for our family to attend a Broadway play when it was her turn to choose the FFA. We live in Texas, so flying to New York for a Broadway play would take too long and cost too much. However, she could choose for us all to see the local high school rendition of *Annie*.

Take these steps to get started:

1. Decide on frequency. How often do you want to try to do an FFA? Unsure? Start monthly and adjust from there.
2. Decide on the rotation order. Try to make this as fair as possible. Maybe you draw names out of a hat, or everyone draws straws cut at different lengths in order to decide the order.
3. Brainstorm a list of ideas for fun family activities. Sit together and list activities you might enjoy doing together as a family. This list will come in handy in the future if someone is feeling uninspired during their turn.
4. Set the date for your first FFA and have the person in charge of this FFA start thinking about what they want to do.

It's that simple. This is such a fun experience for the whole family, especially when you have littles who might be feeling left out as the new stepfamily forms and everyone becomes acclimated to the new culture.

Activity: Introduce Family Fun Activities

Introduce the concept of Family Fun Activities (FFAs) to your family. Brainstorm a list of activities with your family, designate the leader rotation, and schedule your first activity on the calendar!

BONDING WITH YOUR STEPCHILD

There are so many factors that can affect how easy it is to bond with your stepchildren: Their age, your age, how long it has been since their parents split, parental alienation and/or loyalty binds, how much custody time your partner has, and so forth. Yet, despite all these factors, you can still develop a mutually respectful–even enjoyable–relationship with your stepchildren.

Not sure where to start? Here are a few best practices!

Small Pockets of Time

Sometimes, less is more, and developing a relationship with your stepchildren is one of those times. Instead of planning a girls' weekend with your new stepdaughter, opt for a 20-minute trip to the ice-cream shop instead. A lot of things could potentially go wrong in that full weekend. There might be only one or two instances of your stepdaughter acting cranky or seeming unappreciative of all you planned for her … but those one or two episodes can overshadow the rest of the weekend.

The rule of thumb here is quality over quantity. I'd much rather you have a handful of joyful and stress-free memories instead of spending more time together (and possibly more headaches). Stepmom-stepchild relationships are built best on those positive moments. A great place to start is 15–20 minutes of stepmom-stepchild bonding time every other custodial visit.

Low-Pressure Activities

Remember reciprocity? This is one of those times it rears its ugly head if you're not careful. When planning your bonding time with your stepchildren, opt for low-pressure activities. Don't spend too much time, energy, or money on these events because that investment only ups the stakes.

Give only what you can give without expectation.

For some of you, building LEGO kits might be relaxing and a great bonding activity you can do in small time increments with your stepchild. For others of you, building those kits may be stressful because you're in a power struggle over who's going to do the next step, and it's not a pleasurable time at all for either of you.

Choose activities that are typically carefree, stress-free, and joyful. Do you see why that trip to the ice-cream shop works so well?

Most children are happy when they're eating gobs of melting sugar. Take the win.

An Activity They Enjoy

If you aren't sure where to start bonding with your stepchild, I recommend meeting them where they're at.

Does your stepson love video games? Ask if you can sit and watch him play and have him explain to you what's happening as he plays. Then, ask if you can join him after a little while. Even when you get it wrong (like when I ask Krista if she's doing an ascension quest in Genshin Impact every day, which I guess isn't a realistic frequency), you're still showing an interest in them and developing that relationship deeper.

Have a stepdaughter who loves reading? Take her to the library and let her check out as many books as she wants. I used to follow Krista's favorite author on Instagram and show her some of her posts about new books that were releasing soon.

Maybe your stepchild loves crafting. Get a special craft kit or find a fun craft on Pinterest for the two of you to make together.

Do you have teenagers? Download TikTok and send them random videos. Use the new slang in a "cringe" way. (However, and I cannot emphasize this enough, avoid "your mom" jokes if their parent in their other home is their mom ... awkward.)

What matters most is that you're making the effort to connect on their terms–not yours.

Share Something You Enjoyed When You Were Their Age

If you have started developing a relationship with your stepchildren, but their interests don't enable you to join, or they're protective of their interests and don't want you to join, try sharing something with them that you enjoyed when you were their age. However, it is imperative that you check your expectations before taking this step. Your stepchild might reject or mock your interest, so be prepared ahead of time. If you recognize your expectations and won't be able to give in this way without receiving respect in return, skip this suggestion.

When Krista was first learning how to read, I introduced her to *The Boxcar Children*, which was one of my favorite book series growing up. We read the books together at night before bed, and it was a really sweet bonding activity that we both look back on fondly. A few years later, we started watching *Little House on the Prairie* together. I watched the show with my stepmom growing up, and it was a favorite memory. Now Krista has a similar one. When it works, it works.

Shoulder-to-Shoulder Activities

A great way to reduce pressure on bonding with your stepchild is to choose shoulder-to-shoulder activities.[29] Driving in the car, cooking in the kitchen, and playing video games are all great shoulder-to-shoulder activities. Removing the face-to-face component of an activity greatly reduces the pressure. There's no expectation of respectful facial expressions or feeling the need to fill silence.

Activity: Brainstorm Bonding Ideas

Create a list of bonding ideas (per child, if you have more than one!) based on the tips in this chapter. Use the questions below to guide your brainstorming. Not every idea has to be a winner, just write down whatever comes to mind, and rule out ideas later.

DISCIPLINE AS A STEPMOM

One of my favorite stepparent discipline quotes–and where I always start with coaching clients–is "Connection before correction," by Dr. Patricia Papernow.[29] Because kids don't view their stepparents as authority figures, especially early on–unless they were very young when they met–being the disciplinarian usually backfires. Until stepmoms have bonded with their stepchildren and created a respectful, mutual relationship, they shouldn't step into a disciplinarian role.

When a stepmom enters the scene, she begins to pick up any perceived slack. She's read up on parenting best practices, and when she notices gaps at home, she steps in to create structure that sets everyone up for long-term success. While this is great in theory, the unfortunate reality is, the parent and children may not be ready for that change. When and how you introduce stepparent discipline to your dynamic can make a world of difference to its success.

I remember, as a child of divorce, when my stepdad would punish me, I would hold a grudge much longer than if my mom had doled out the same punishment. I hadn't built that relationship with him, and as a result, punishment wasn't well received. The stepmom-stepchild relationship is already precarious, so don't take on discipline or punishment until that bond is strong enough to withstand it. If you push discipline as a stepmom too soon, you're opening the door to the dreaded "You're not my mom!" retort.

Getting Started Disciplining

First, let your partner take the lead. This can be a tough one for many independent stepmoms, but it's important to follow your partner's lead when it comes to parenting your stepchildren. Your partner knows their children best, and you can learn from an "observe first, parent later" approach. You might be surprised that some of their laissez-faire approach is actually intentional.

Not only does taking the backseat give you time to learn the current culture and expectations, but it also allows time to build that respectful relationship with your stepchildren necessary for taking that next step.

Then, once you've successfully built the foundation of your relationship with your stepchildren and feel prepared to take on more parenting, your partner should initiate the conversation. It's crucial that your partner elevates you to your stepchildren and makes it clear that when you enforce a rule, it's the same as if your partner was saying it. It may seem superfluous or obvious, but you shouldn't assume that your stepchildren see you as an equal parenting figure, especially if your stepchildren aren't very young.

I often recommend having this conversation in a family meeting and reviewing the house rules while you're discussing expectations and discipline. Refer to Chapter 2 if you need a refresher!

Discipline Engagement Scale

Once you decide to be involved in disciplining your stepchildren, you still have a big decision to make. How involved do you want to be? How comfortable do you feel being involved in this way? That answer will vary from stepmom to stepmom! And it could even change throughout your journey as a stepmom, as your role and relationship with your stepchild evolves.

I like to think of discipline as a scale (Figure 5.2). You can be completely involved in discipline or completely disengaged ... or somewhere in the middle! A completely disengaged on discipline stepmom

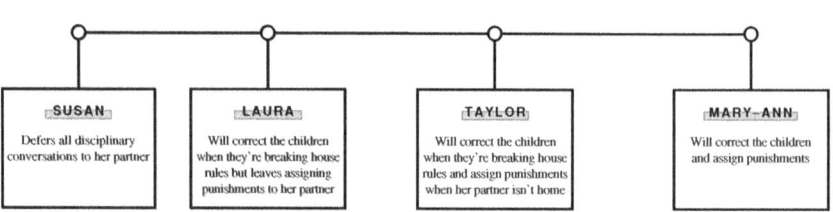

Figure 5.2   Discipline engagement scale with examples.

will defer all corrective and disciplinary conversations to her partner. A completely involved on discipline stepmom is comfortable correcting her stepchildren, enforcing rules, and assigning punishments.

A stepmom who's about a four on a scale of one to ten (Laura) might feel comfortable correcting her stepchildren but leaves the punishing to her partner. This way, she doesn't have to be the messenger of the worst part! A stepmom who's about a seven on the scale (Taylor) might feel comfortable correcting her stepchildren and will also issue a punishment when her partner isn't home, resulting in her being the only adult home. But she leaves the punishing to her partner when they are home.

There's no singularly correct answer for how to discipline or how involved you should be with punishments. It's dependent on the relationship you have with your stepchildren, their ages, how long you've been in their lives, and other factors like their trauma, their relationship with your partner, how supportive your partner is of you disciplining them, and more. I'd recommend you err on the side of less disciplining and punishing, but do what feels right and aligned within your family. No two stepfamilies are alike!

Enforcing Rules

So, you've decided that you want to enforce rules in your home? Amazing! Let's help you do it as effectively and peacefully as possible. Because what is your top priority as a stepmom? Protecting your peace!

A good rule of thumb for balancing peace and responsibility is to give yourself a maximum of two times of enforcing the rules before you step back and let your partner take over. Ask the child kindly for whatever you need to be done, and if you continue to get pushback from them, you can ask again. But if the resistance continues or the child becomes disrespectful, you should let your partner step in. If your partner isn't home, you can wait on the discipline until your partner is home. Let the child know they can discuss it with their parent when they return, and you should disengage from the child for a bit.

If your stepchild is determined to disrespect you and not see you as an authority figure, it isn't worth losing your peace. This is the perfect opportunity to disengage, support your partner, and wash your hands of anything outside of your control. (More on this in Chapter 8, I promise!)

Having a stepchild that doesn't listen to you or respect you doesn't mean that you've failed as a stepmom or that you're not doing it right. Don't take any of this personally. Your stepchildren have been through a lot of change and emotions they don't fully understand, and they could have difficulty coping and managing those emotions. Further, they could be facing loyalty binds with their other parent, and obeying you may feel like disobeying their other parent.[30] It can feel like an impossible situation with no right answers.

If you've followed the steps provided and still aren't able to enforce rules or discipline your stepchildren without pushback, it's very likely not about you at all. That's okay! Consider yourself relieved of the duty for now. Focus on building a positive relationship with them outside of disciplinary actions.

Activity: Identify Your Desired Discipline Involvement Level
Think about your relationship with your stepchild and how involved you want to be with discipline. Where do you want to fall on the discipline engagement scale, as portrayed in Figure 5.3?

In this chapter, I gave you the tools to build your stepmom role from top to bottom. At this point, you should be crystal clear on what you want to do in your stepfamily, what you want your impact to be, and the fact that you should be unapologetic about your chosen role. A well-defined role is such a great start, but it's not the whole picture. To get the most out of your role and have it be the most fulfilling, you must balance the stepmom part of your role with the rest

Where do you want to fall on the discipline engagement scale?

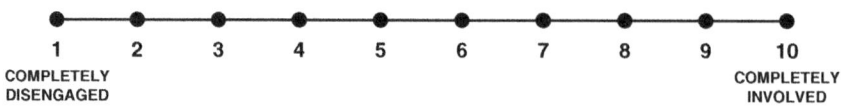

1   2   3   4   5   6   7   8   9   10
COMPLETELY   **COMPLETELY**
DISENGAGED   **INVOLVED**

STEPMOMMING.COM

Figure 5.3   Discipline engagement scale.

of your life and those other things that make you uniquely who you are. I named my business Stepmomming because it's such an important reminder: Stepmomming is what we do, stepmom is not all of who we are. In the next chapter, I'll dive deep into the process of balancing your identity and interests to help sidestep burnout.

CHAPTER 6

Balance Self-Fulfillment

Redefining your role to better align yourself with your values and desires and to create relational reciprocity allows room for balanced self-fulfillment. You're now ready to compartmentalize the stepmom part of your identity and find balance in all areas of your life. You were so much more before you became a stepmom, and you mustn't lose that sense of self. This chapter addresses some of the most common obstacles to a peaceful mindset: resentment, identity confusion, and burnout.

Resentment is one of the most prevalent struggles I see with my stepmom clients. This stepmomming gig is so much harder than anyone anticipated, and it's virtually impossible to not let that reality spiral into resentment. But I have hope, my friend! Resentment is not a fact of life. Once you can recognize where your resentment originates from and then set appropriate boundaries to protect yourself, you can find freedom from your resentful thoughts.

A common trigger my clients identify that contributes to their resentment is the difference in how they spend time after becoming a stepmom, as compared to before. Many of you go all-in on your roles and dive headfirst into all things family. When this happens, however, you often lose so much of what makes you truly you. You might even experience what feels like an identity crisis.[31] In this chapter, you'll learn how to reclaim your identity, balancing who you were before with your stepmom role, which provides you with a much more well-rounded life experience.

Another unfortunate byproduct of diving headfirst into stepmomming is burnout. Working overtime to prove yourself as a stepmom is a surefire way to feel overworked and underappreciated. This chapter also explores the very real health impact of burnout and its root causes. You'll learn how to avoid the long-term unmanaged stress that causes burnout by incorporating practical suggestions backed by science into your life.

Resolving resentment, identity concerns, and burnout will greatly enhance your peace of mind. It directly relates to your self-fulfillment, feeling more balanced as a stepmom, and beyond. Stepmomming cannot consume all your thoughts and energy. You are so much more than this role.

Resolving Resentment

"Holding on to anger is like drinking poison and expecting the other person to die."[32]

– Buddha

In previous chapters, you learned to work through the important concepts of mourning the family life that you thought you'd have and the role of reciprocity in stepfamily relationships. So, this chapter may feel a bit repetitive. But if you have felt resentful at any point in your stepmom journey, I want to ensure that I visit these topics through this lens as well. Every stepmom that I've ever met has expressed the following at some point: "This is not what I signed up for!" "This was supposed to be easier!" or "I deserve better than this!" In short, every stepmom I have ever met has felt resentful at some point in her journey.

My friend Beth McDonough states it best, "Resentment grows in the gap between expectation and reality."[33] When your expectations are not met, you experience feelings of disappointment, frustration, and sometimes anger. When expectations are repeatedly not met, resentment then festers. Sometimes, this is an innocuous, simple expectation, such as "I expect not to see family photos of my partner's first family." But when you visit your in-laws and come face-to-face with those photos, you begin to feel like an outsider, unwelcome and uncomfortable. Repeatedly visiting your in-laws enables your resentment to grow–not because of your partner's parents but because of their home decor.

Sometimes, it feels like an even bigger intrusion, such as when your partner's ex uses their old house key to enter your home. You might think, "I expect that my partner's ex will not let themselves into my home." And yet, when this person lets themselves in to gather the children during a custody exchange or walks in with your step-child while you're not home to gather a belonging they've forgotten, you're appalled, angry, and feel unsafe in your own home. Expecting someone who doesn't live in your home, to not let themselves in unannounced feels like a normal, reasonable expectation. But your current reality isn't your expectation, and thus you feel resentment.

Expectations originate from two main sources: core values and relational reciprocity. As I detailed in Chapter 2, your core values are such a natural part of you that when violated, they cause an immediate visceral reaction. Repeated attacks on your core values inevitably lead to bitterness. Additionally, when you don't see reciprocity in your relationships, you experience resentment.

One of the pitfalls of having core values is assuming that others feel the same way and that they will honor your values. It's natural to expect kindness, respect, communication, and appreciation. Those are reasonable values. And yet, in a stepfamily, everyone has different values, different perspectives, and thus, different interpretations of those values.

Imagine you took your stepdaughter to the nail salon with you. Say that you had a great day bonding, letting her get the nails of her dreams: dip powder, special shape, and hand-painted designs. It cost you a small fortune, but it was worth it for the memories. Your partner fully endorsed and encouraged the outing. You were on cloud nine ... until your stepdaughter came home from her other parent's home a week later with her nails stripped bare again. You felt completely disrespected and unappreciated. Your feelings are valid. Your core values of respect and appreciation have been violated, and your expectations of those core values being met vary from your reality. Naturally, you begin to feel resentful. But if you explore the other parent's perspective of this same event, it's likely that they felt disrespected and acted out accordingly. They expected such bonding experiences to be reserved for them and their child, not with a stepparent. Both of you have a core value of respect and expectations of that core value being honored that feel reasonable to each of you. But these perspectives and expectations are in conflict.

Here's one more core value example to validate a common example I come across with my coaching clients. Many of the stepmoms I work with are very organized and thrive with structure. In fact, one of their primary core values is structure. These are the stepmoms who know the parenting plan forward and backward; they can tell you differences of the regular custody schedule versus the holiday one without consulting the order. They know which parent is responsible for healthcare expenses and who pays for school supplies this year. So, when their partner and their stepchild's other parent consistently alter the schedule and swap random nights or weekends, the stepmom is left feeling triggered. Her core value of structure hasn't been honored, resulting in her no longer feeling safe or at peace. When this becomes a recurring issue, she begins to feel resentful toward her partner, the other parent, and eventually even the children, for repeatedly making her feel unsafe and imbalanced.

A lack of reciprocity, as detailed in Chapter 5, can also lead to resentment. Giving more than you are receiving in your stepfamily relationships isn't sustainable. When you feel like you aren't seeing acknowledgment, appreciation, or any other return on your investment, you will feel taken for granted, jealous, frustrated, overwhelmed, burned out, and eventually, resentful. Imagine your stepchild complains about the dinner you cook nearly every single evening. Behind the scenes, you make sure the pantry is stocked with their favorite foods before every custody transition, are intentional about balanced nutrition, and keep meals that have been a hit in the past in the rotation coinciding with custody time. Your partner hasn't had to lift a finger to help with grocery planning, shopping, or cooking for as long as you can remember. It worked well for your family, until it didn't. Once your stepchild started complaining, you no longer had reciprocity for these actions. You were being intentional, thoughtful, and taking time daily to do something for them. Yet when they stopped appreciating it and started vocalizing their displeasure, you stopped receiving a return on your investment. This recurring imbalance between what you are giving and what you are receiving eventually leads to resentment.

I always recommend a two-part approach when dealing with triggers and resentment. First, you must remove the triggers. Then, you need to find and address the root cause behind the resentment. If you can easily spot the triggers (e.g., my partner's ex lets themselves into our home), great! You're ready to move on to removing the triggers. If they're a bit more subtle or there's a lot happening simultaneously and it's harder to pinpoint, I suggest that you keep a journal. In it, you should write down every time you feel triggered. When they're all in a list, it's easier to recognize themes.

If you notice that your resentment grows each time that you start working on your grocery list for your custodial time, take note of it. In addition, also take note of the uneasiness and tension you begin to feel when you start pulling out ingredients to cook, or the breath you hold when you place your stepchild's dinner plate on the table in front of them and prepare for feedback. Once you can pinpoint that dinnertime is your trigger, stop cooking. You can actively work to limit this resentment by limiting the triggers.

Once the cloud of anger or frustration from those triggers is removed, you're in a better headspace to analyze the root cause. In this example, it's the lack of appreciation and the felt disrespect. It's easier to share with your partner, "I'm feeling like my efforts aren't appreciated, and when complaints are made about how I didn't do something 'right,' I feel disrespected" than to have them understand what you need when you try to express "I get frustrated when my stepchild complains about their dinner." The issue isn't that they are complaining about dinner; that's a symptom of the larger problem. You don't need your partner to fix the dinner issue–well, actually, you do, but you really need them to address the larger problem of appreciation and respect. Your core values need to be protected, and you need reciprocity in your relationships.

Activity: Keep a Trigger Journal

Grab a notebook or create a new note on your phone and give it three columns. The columns should be titled: Triggering Event, Source, and Core Value. In the first column, you'll write what happened: your stepchild complained about lunch. In the second column, clarify if the trigger source is violation of a core value or lack of reciprocity. If your answer for source was core value, then in the third column, you'll journal about which core value(s) were violated.

When you have a bit of mental clarity and peace from the conflict, take a look at your journal. What themes do you see? Are any core values repeatedly being violated? Where are you missing reciprocity? Which tasks do you need to step back from? This trigger journal can be so insightful when you have the ability and time to analyze it.

Rediscovering Your Identity

"The most courageous act is still to think for yourself. Aloud."[34]
– Coco Chanel, fashion designer and businesswoman

I want to take a trip down memory lane for a bit. I had sold my home to move in with my then-fiancé/now-husband, Kevin, and his daughter, Krista, in his hometown, a town I was unfamiliar with about 30 minutes away from my home. Logistically, it made sense for our family. Krista wouldn't have to change schools, and it was closer to the building in which Kevin and I worked. Emotionally, I was distraught. I had worked so hard to be able to purchase my first home. I decorated it from nothing. I grew and matured in that home. I became a truly independent woman for the first time in that home. And I sold it all to become a full-time partner and part-time stepmom.

With that move, I was no longer servicing my tutoring clients because the drive didn't make sense from my new town. I rarely saw my sister and my young nephew because they, too, lived close to my old home, and I was enveloped in adjusting to my new role and my new family.

One day I looked in the mirror, and I simply didn't recognize myself. I felt uprooted and disoriented. I had stopped doing so many of the things I loved, and instead I became wholly a stepmom. I was experiencing an "identity crisis," and I needed help.[31]

READJUSTING YOUR ROLE

I soon realized that I had adjusted my schedule, my social outings, my job, my home, my *everything* to become a part of this step-family. Not because my partner had asked me to, but because I wanted to prove I was all-in. I wanted to prove the value I could add to this family. I wanted to be the best partner and stepmom I could be. (Remember our discussion on overachievers in Chapter 5? Guilty!) But by going all-in as a stepmom, I had stopped doing the things I love–the things that made me, *me*.

Once I realized I no longer recognized myself, I began the process of stepping back, redefining the stepmom I want to be, and rebalancing my role. I explained to my partner how I was feeling and how I needed to balance who I was with the new family I was joining, and he was completely supportive.

We then worked together to identify which tasks I could pass back over to him, and I started scheduling time for the things I had loved before I became a stepmom: visits to my sister's home, wine nights with my best friend, and fitness boot camp three times per week. The more I stepped back from the stepmom role I'd been all-consumed by, and the more I started balancing the individual I am with the family I'm in, the more well-rounded and fulfilled I became.

Further, as I shifted from being an all-in stepmom I hardly recognized to a balanced woman who was also a stepmom, I felt a transformation beginning. I felt a weight lifting off my shoulders–the pressure to be the perfect stepmom and partner was drifting away. I felt renewed in my purpose and rejuvenated as a parent and partner.

I hadn't realized how drained and burned out I'd become trying to play this part full-time. Taking time for the things I loved outside of being a stepmom fully rejuvenated me. I was equally excited about the time I was home with the family and the time I spent doing things for myself.

The tagline of my business is, "Stepmomming is what you do, it's not who you are." This tagline was built as a result of this identity crisis I'd experienced when stepmomming had become my entire identity, instead of one of the things I do–one of many parts of me.

When I shifted stepmomming to something I do, my whole world shifted. I was a visibly happier person, but I also became an infinitely better stepmom. Now full of energy and enthusiasm, I built my partner up and supported him, letting him know I trust him instead of taking over all the tasks for our household. I also gave my husband and stepdaughter much-needed time alone to strengthen their bond.

SELF-CARE BEFORE YOU NEED IT

I see many clients, especially childless stepmoms, who face the same identity crisis I did. My advice is always the same: Take a step back, take time for yourself, and then continue taking time for yourself. In fact, my advice for all stepmoms is to practice self-care early and often. Even before you realize you need it, if you can.

Self-care looks different for everyone. For some, it's a mani-pedi with a glass of rosé; for others, it's curling up on the back porch with a good book. For you, it might be yoga class or journaling. Find what fills you up, what calms you, and what rejuvenates you, and then, do it!

It's not too late to address and correct your identity crisis. You're not beyond recognition or beyond help. Take a step back, revel in the transformation, and then make self-care a daily routine. Remember: Stepmomming is what you do, it's not who you are.

Activity: Create a List of What Rejuvenates You

Make a list of activities that recharge you or bring you joy. They can be big like having a spa day, or something small like drinking your cup of coffee while it's hot, calling your mom, or going for a walk.

It's important to keep this list somewhere easily accessible so you know how to use your free time wisely! Instead of doom scrolling when you have an hour before your partner and stepchildren get home from baseball practice, choose something from your self-care list to make the most of your down time!

Activity: Schedule Your Self-Care

For this activity, schedule self-care three times in the next week. Remember: Not all self-care is time-intensive. Vary the time commitment of your chosen activities so you don't feel extra stress from what's supposed to be stress-relieving. Make those self-care appointments as nonnegotiable on your calendar as possible.

Overcoming Burnout

Stepmoms suffer from intense burnout. You dive headfirst into your family, giving sacrificially and putting your family's needs before your own. You give repeatedly, even when there's nothing left in you to give. You run yourself ragged and hit a breaking point of burnout.

Not to be dramatic, but burnout (or long-term unmanaged stress) will literally kill you. Stress affects the immune system, digestive system, and hormones.[35] Human bodies are equipped to manage this strain on a periodic basis but not for extended time periods. You're simply not built for constant burnout. That's why it's imperative to learn how to manage stress, and complete the stress response cycle, as Drs. Emily and Amelia Nagoski coined it.[36]

The first step toward relieving burnout and stress on your body is recognizing that the stress is different from the stressors. You don't have the same stressors today that your ancestors did generations ago, but you still experience the same stress response to today's stressors. Just like your ancestors would've experienced stress if they were being charged by a hippopotamus, you still experience that same fight-or-flight response. Your heart still races; your body still focuses on safety above all else when faced with modern stressors.

Bills will still come next month, dinner will still need made every night, your custody schedule will continue to oscillate between your house and your stepchild's other home, and your partner's child (and likely also their ex) will always be part of your lives. Stressors will always exist. But the good news is that you don't need to eliminate the stressors to eliminate stress (and subsequent burnout).[37]

It's not actually the stressors that are causing burnout. It's the unmanaged stress! When your body stays in a state of unresolved stress, it impairs your ability to be present, engaged, and peaceful. In fact, solving a problem (i.e., paying a bill, making dinner, your stepchildren returning to their other home for the week) doesn't resolve the stress. Your body doesn't know it's safe yet. You must complete the stress response cycle.[36] Drs. Emily and Amelia Nagoski give us a number of ways to complete the stress response cycle and give your body the release it needs:

- **Physical Activity**

  Go for a run or a swim, attend a yoga class or do Pilates, lift weights, or climb stairs. The type of activity doesn't matter; you just need to get moving enough so that you begin to breathe deeply. Because you feel stress most days, you'll want to get your body moving 20–60 minutes per day most days too. My mind is always clearer during the weeks I've prioritized attending my workout classes. As much as the lazy part of me would love to chalk that up to a coincidence, of course it isn't.

- **Deep Breaths**

  If you can't sneak away for a run, you can still take good deep breaths. Breathing deeply and slowly lowers your body's stress activation. My favorite deep breathing technique is box breathing: Picture a box or find something square in your room, breathe in through your nose for four counts as you work your way up the side of the square, hold for four counts as you work your way across the top of the square, breathe out through your mouth for the same count as you move your eyes down the right side of the square, and then hold your breath again for four counts as you complete the square along the bottom edge. Continue taking breaths in this way until you feel your body calming and the stress leaving.[38]

- **Positive Social Interaction**

  Social interaction is an indicator to your body that your world is safe. You can let your guard down and relieve your stress; you're not in danger (of the charging hippo, or your partner's high-conflict ex). The world is good, and you are safe. That's right: Science supports girls' night. Text your friends and get something on the books. It's for your health!

- **Laughter**

  I did a presentation in my college speech class about how laughter is the best medicine, and it truly is. Laughter is a great way to physically relieve your body of the stress it's holding onto, and to flood your body with positive feelings instead. Sometimes when I'm in my head about a stressor, I'll ask Krista to send me funny Reels on Instagram, or suggest we watch old episodes of America's Funniest Home Videos as a family. It distracts me from the stressor and completes my stress response cycle.

◆ **Affection**

On days when I'm feeling overwhelmed, I'll often look at Kevin and ask, "May I have a hug please?" because his hugs signal to me that I'm safe, I'm capable, and I'm not alone. And it doesn't just work for me! A safe, warm hug with someone you trust is the equivalent for relieving stress of jogging a couple of miles.[39]

◆ **Crying**

Do you ever just need to let yourself cry to feel a release? I certainly do. Your body intuitively knows that crying is a way to relieve your body of stress it's carrying.

◆ **Creative Expression**

For Christmas a couple of years ago, Kevin bought me an adult coloring book featuring phrases with swear words in it. After an especially bad day at work, I love to sit down with my markers and color away my stress. If you want to relieve stress, find ways to express yourself creatively: writing, singing, dancing, making art, and so on.

All these suggestions have one thing in common: action. You must actually *do* something. You can't tell yourself that you are safe and all is well. "Completing the cycle isn't an intellectual decision; it's a physiological shift."[40] Regularly complete the stress cycle and overcome burnout.

Activity: Implement Stress Response Solutions

Review this list of methods to complete the stress response cycle:

- ◆ Physical Activity
- ◆ Deep Breaths
- ◆ Positive Social Interaction
- ◆ Laughter
- ◆ Affection

◆ Crying
◆ Creative Expression

Schedule physical activity most days on your calendar. Keep a list of the activities that resonated with you somewhere else easily accessible to consult when you need to relieve yourself of stress and signal to your body that you are safe.

In many ways, this was an emotionally heavy chapter: resentment, burnout, identity crises. But these are very real threats to your peace as a stepmom, and they must be addressed. My hope is by this point you've begun resolving the biggest obstacles to self-fulfillment and have a clear idea of the balance you desire in your life. After all that intentional time spent on you, it's time to shift your focus to your partner and building an unshakable relationship. They're the reason that you're a stepmom after all. In the next chapter, I'll share my favorite tools and insights to create the strongest, most meaningful bond possible.

CHAPTER 7

Cultivate an Unshakable Relationship

You are reading this book because you fell in love with someone incredible. Please don't let all the other drama cloud that joyful fact. Admittedly, there are a lot of complexities and complications with relationships like ours, but there's a lot of beauty in them too.

In this chapter, I'll share with you all my favorite tools for creating an unshakable bond with your partner. Many of the tools center on healthy communication, but others focus on connection and showing your love to your partner well. You two are the foundation of your family, and it's imperative it's a solid foundation.

Your significant other is your partner. Your lover. Your teammate. Your friend. They are the person who is worth fighting through the muck for.

One day, the kids will be gone and moved out of the house. There won't be a custody schedule or child support. You'll interact with the other parent sparingly. But what will remain if you've done it right? Your relationship with your partner. This substantial chapter contains eight different lessons. If that doesn't underscore the importance of the topic, I'm not sure what will.

I am passionate about helping stepcouples overcome the abysmal divorce rates for marriages like ours and find lasting peace and happiness. I'm tired of seeing bitter exes, hurt and confused stepchildren, and unjust legal systems ripping apart couples. I'm done hearing, "If it weren't for the stepfamily stuff, our relationship would be perfect!" This chapter is devoted to helping you protect your relationship from the drama by ensuring it's as strong as possible.

You deserve a stepmom life you love. You deserve a happy, healthy relationship you love. Let's get started!

How to Pick Your Battles

"You don't have to attend every argument you're invited to."
— Unknown

One of the most cliché pieces of marriage advice out there is to pick your battles. It wouldn't be widely advised if it lacked merit. Yet the reality as a stepmom is, there are so many triggers that it can overwhelm you to the point you want to choose *every* battle. Every battle feels threatening and worth fighting. I don't know your exact situation, but I do know that not every battle needs to be fought.

To help you determine which battles matter most and deserve your time, attention, and energy, I've created a list of four questions to ask yourself. The answers to these questions will help you determine if conflict resolution with your partner is necessary, or if another path would be better advised.

QUESTION #1: IS THIS ISSUE RECURRING?

If this is an issue that has occurred multiple times and it triggers you each time, it might be a battle worth choosing. Repeated triggering isn't going to be healthy or productive for your relationship. So, if the health or longevity of your relationship is at stake, it's likely worth taking a stand and working with your partner to find resolution.

A few years ago, I had the privilege of working with a sweet stepmom with a heart of gold. She loves her husband deeply, but even after seven years together, Cassie was still struggling in her role. She needed a combination of internal confidence and her partner's support and healthy boundaries with his ex to settle into her role.

Every time her stepchildren came to Cassie's house, they came with a bag full of clothes packed from their other home. While some might see this as a generous act, Cassie took it very personally.

She thought it meant that her family members didn't trust her to provide adequate clothing for them in her home.

Is this something that, as Cassie's coach, I wanted her to be able to move past without addressing? Yes! I wanted her to recognize that it wasn't personal at all–and even if it was, no one else's opinion of her matters. But she was too deep into her insecurities to pull herself out of it and have the same perspective I could. So before asking her to reframe how she sees the clothing-filled luggage, I helped her to outline a conversation she needed to have with her partner who's the best person to help protect her from her triggers.

Because his children brought a suitcase with them every other weekend, Cassie was feeling repeatedly hurt and frustrated. It was also the first thing she saw when they walked in the door, and that luggage set an antagonistic tone for their time together. Because it was a recurring issue that was dramatically affecting her peace, it was a battle worth picking.

On the other hand, if it's something that has only happened once, or is a very rare unique situation, it's likely not a battle worth fighting ... until it recurs.

I'll encourage you to finish reading and ask yourself the rest of the questions before making a final decision on the best course of action.

QUESTION #2: WILL THIS MATTER IN THE FUTURE?

One of the best questions you can ask yourself if you're faced with conflict is if this issue will matter in the future. If it won't, then why are you allowing it to cost you your peace? A widely shared tool in the mental health world is the 5 × 5 Rule. Though I cannot find who originally penned the rule, it reads something like this: If something will not matter in five years, then do not spend more than five minutes worrying about it.[41] It's a powerful perspective, isn't it?

My client, Trisha, had a stepchild diagnosed with Oppositional Defiant Disorder (ODD). His behavior, especially when his dad wasn't around, was becoming unbearable for Trisha. I asked her, "If this behavior continues, what will things look like in five years?" and she sadly admitted she thought she would be divorced. Trisha didn't feel respected in her home. It was like she was constantly walking on eggshells, waiting for the next argument to occur. It created ongoing tension with her husband that very quickly was building into resentment. The viability of their relationship depended on this issue being addressed, so it became an easy "Yes, this is a battle worth picking!"

QUESTION #3: WHICH OF MY PARTNER'S CORE VALUES IS MOTIVATING THEIR BEHAVIOR RIGHT NOW?

Always assume positive intent from your partner. It's important to always remember two things: Your partner wants you to feel protected and respected, and your partner is always doing the best they can. While their best might look different or less than what you'd like to see, it is their best, nonetheless.

You've learned about the power of core values. If you're stuck in a position where you think you might need to choose a battle with your partner, I want you to first reflect on their core values. What might be motivating them to act the way they are? Knowing this will help you assume positive intent.

For example, one of my clients, Becca, came to me, frustrated with her partner dragging his feet on downloading the co-parenting app that she had researched. She knew that the app would resolve scheduling and communication issues, and she was frustrated that her partner seemed to not appreciate her time and energy spent researching. She wanted him to protect her by mitigating conflict with her stepchildren's other parent, and she felt betrayed by his inaction.

But her partner's top core value is financial security. He very much appreciated her problem-solving and her research, but he was rendered immobile by the payment section of the website every time he went to register for the app. He thought there must be a cheaper (or better, free) solution. And because the value he holds most dear is financial security, he would rather have conflict with his co-parent than have an extra expense that threatened their financial security.

Once Becca could empathize with the core value motivating her husband, she had more clarity on whether this was a battle worth picking, and if so, how to approach it.

If you still can't determine the motivation based on their primary core values, then revisit Chapter 1 about your partner's perspective and see if something strikes a chord.

QUESTION #4: IS THERE ANOTHER WAY I CAN PROTECT MY PEACE RIGHT NOW, WITHOUT PICKING THIS BATTLE?

Before choosing to bring the issue up to your partner, consider first if there's another way you can protect your peace. My friend Jenni does this well. Instead of confronting her partner every time her stepchildren don't clean their bathroom as agreed upon, she closes the door to their bathroom so she can't see how dirty it is and become triggered. Her peace matters more.

If it feels like you are inundated with stressors and are feeling completely overwhelmed, I get it. As your coach, I would rather you fight more battles than less, if you're unsure if an issue should be brought up to your partner or not. They aren't mind readers, and they'll never know if something is affecting you until you tell them. As you begin to feel more comfortable and less triggered, you'll open space to be more prudent with these decisions.

But an important caveat: Err on the side of more conversations, as long as they are productive and effective.

Activity: Practice Choosing Your Battles

Consider the last battle you chose to fight with your partner. What are your answers to the four questions: Is this issue recurring? Will this matter in the future? Which of my partner's core values is motivating their behavior right now? Is there another way I can protect my peace right now, without picking this battle? Would you still have decided to initiate the discussion with your partner? If so, how could you have approached the conversation differently?

The Art of Kind Communication

> *"The act of not choosing kindness is therefore doubly hurtful—to our partners and to ourselves—because it undercuts our efforts for growth and the potential for greater intimacy."*[42]
>
> – Sanaa Hyder, MSEd, psychotherapist

When I first met Kevin, I was not great at communicating. I wasn't even *good* at it. Growing up, my examples of communication were passive-aggressive or aggressive-aggressive. I tended to yell to get my point across, become defensive easily, and (I'm ashamed to admit) try to hurt my partner with my words as an unhealthy reaction. Poor communication can damage your relationship–sometimes beyond repair. But healthy, respectful communication strengthens and deepens it.

Several years ago, I moderated a panel of stepmom experts discussing communication tips for couples. My mentor, Jenna Korf, said something so simple but so profound on this call that it stuck with me all these years later. She said, "Talk to your partner like they're the person you love most in this world." Even when you disagree, your communication needs to be kind. If a core value has been violated or you're feeling threatened, your partner still deserves your respect. No matter what is going on outside of it, your relationship needs to be protected. This means no name calling, no underhanded digs, and no bringing up past transgressions. If you're not in a place to speak kindly to your partner, take a beat and return to the conversation when you can speak to them as if they're the person you love most in this world, because, after all, they are.

You can further strengthen a foundation of kindness for your relationship by always assuming positive intent. You might not always understand why your partner chooses to act a certain way or what their words mean, but you know they don't ever intend to hurt you. They would not intentionally choose to upset you. Assume positive intentions are behind their actions and seek to understand before jumping to conclusions. Ask your partner kindly what their motivations and intentions were and ask clarifying questions if you still don't understand. If helpful, say something like, "I know you wouldn't intentionally make me feel [not prioritized/disrespected/ignored/etc.], but I'm struggling to understand [describe the action that upset you]. Can you help me see your perspective on what happened?" This question is non-accusatory and invites your partner to share their intent in a way that encourages connection over defensiveness.

It's important to note that you and your partner may not be able to understand each other's perspectives. Try as you might, you'll never be in their exact shoes, and vice versa. You're in the same family with the same key players, but the dynamics affect each of you differently. Just because your partner cannot understand your perspective (or you, theirs) doesn't negate the validity of your experience. If you reach an impasse in a conversation where your partner is unable to understand your perspective, seek validation instead of understanding. Try saying something like, "You may not fully understand my perspective, and that's okay. But I do need you to respect that this is my experience, and it matters." Prioritize connection when true empathy and full understanding aren't possible.

My final note on kind communication is a distinction originally noted by Dr. John Gottman, a bestselling author and one of the premier experts on marriage in the world. He warns couples against criticism, which he defines as globally attacking your partner's character or personality.[43] One example would be telling your partner, "You're so selfish! You never think of anyone but yourself!" in response to them forgetting to let you know about a custody swap. You have every right to be upset by their mistake but criticizing them is not the correct way to address it. Dr. Gottman warns that criticism is a slippery slope to contempt, treating your partner as if they're below you. This is especially worrisome because contempt is the single greatest predictor of divorce.[44] Consistently speaking unkindly toward and about your partner, to the point that you begin to look down on them from a place of superiority, will all but guarantee an end to your relationship. If that's not motivation to communicate healthier, I'm not sure what is!

An improvement over criticism is complaints, or negative comments about a specific action or behavior. Complaints might sound like, "I don't like it when you make decisions without letting me know." This is certainly an improvement from the criticism before, but it's not perfect. Many of us use complaints and think they're okay, because we've framed them as "I" statements (focusing on how a behavior impacts us, instead of focusing on what our partner did wrong). But the negative emotion behind the complaint still leaves your partner feeling defensive.

The kindest way you can communicate with your partner is with a request, or a positive statement about a behavior change that you desire. In our custody swap example, a request might be, "I would like it if you would let me know within an hour of agreeing to custody schedule adjustments, so I can plan dinner and activities accordingly." The key here is understanding that a request is not a command. Your partner doesn't have to honor your request (but hopefully they will). When they feel respected and you approach them with kindness, seeking to compromise and work together on a solution, they're more willing to have a productive conversation with you. They won't feel defensive and shut down the conversation before a meaningful resolution.

Kind communication can literally make or break your relationship. Choose kindness, understanding, and teamwork over ego and emotion. Your partner wants you to feel respected, protected, and loved. Let your words reflect the same intentions back to them.

Activity: Plan for Kinder Communication

Reflect on how your communication can be kinder. Identify any skills from this chapter you want to continue to develop and how you can use them in your interactions. Keep this list nearby as a reminder of the growth you seek.

Activity: Put It in Action

Start recognizing when your communication isn't as kind as it could be, then apologize to your partner and try again.

Mastering the Five Love Languages

"Love is not just a feeling; it's an action."[45]
– Gary Chapman, PhD, author, speaker, and
marriage counselor

Kevin and I lived about 30 minutes from each other when we first began dating. We saw each other as often as we could between our various commitments, but I always craved more time with him. I remember one afternoon he was driving across the metroplex to the military base for his weekend duty with the Texas Air National Guard, and I was a short detour from his route. I invited him over to hang out for a couple of hours, but he declined the offer. He said something to the effect of, "It's not worth it to drive out of the way for only an hour or two hanging out."

This was in our relationship's early days, so naturally I questioned if he was really into me. Of course it's worth it. I'd drive the hour round trip to his house from mine, if it meant I got to see him for even half an hour. In hindsight, there was a lot of context that I was missing from his decision, and I certainly misinterpreted what he said and how he meant it. He was so into me; he knew we'd have a lifetime together (*swoon*), and he simply needed to get to work that day.

But this miscommunication and misunderstanding that caused one of our first disconnects as a couple illustrates a life-changing, marriage-saving concept that you need to know to succeed. It might seem obvious, but intentional connection is necessary for a lasting relationship with your partner. Your relationship requires regular nurturing that is fulfilling for both of you.

If you've ever felt like you're pouring so much into your relationship and not getting what you need to feel connected with your partner in return, you might be speaking different love languages. Dr. Gary Chapman discovered this concept and introduced it in his book, *The 5 Love Languages: The Secret to Love That Lasts*, and it has transformed the lives of countless couples since.[45]

The book's premise is we all need to feel loved by and connected to those around us, but the primary way we feel most loved or connected to someone may vary. In fact, he has identified five different love languages: Acts of Service, Quality Time, Words of Affirmation, Receiving Gifts, and Physical Touch.

Everyone will resonate with all five on some level, but one or two of them likely will hit a bit deeper. Understanding your partner's primary love language and speaking it regularly will ensure that your partner feels that you're invested in your relationship and their satisfaction. Let's review each of these languages, and identify your primary (and secondary, if close) love language. Consider what might be your partner's love language. What lights them up? When have they been most responsive to you? What might have caused that? In what ways does your partner seem to communicate their love to you the most frequently?

ACTS OF SERVICE

Acts of Service means doing things to make your partner's life easier or better. Someone with an Acts of Service primary love language feels most connected to you when you've made them a hot cup of coffee just the way they like it, vacuumed the family room, or taken care of something on their to-do list.

Examples of Acts of Service:
- Make your partner breakfast in bed.
- Take the dog for a walk.
- Fold and put away the laundry.
- Give them an hour of uninterrupted TV time.
- Ask if they want a snack or drink while you're up.
- Let your partner sleep in.
- Wash your partner's car (inside and out).
- Cook their favorite meal.
- Make their side of the bed.
- Draw them a hot bath.
- Mow the lawn or have it mowed.
- Fill the gas tank in your partner's car.
- Give your partner the "night off" and tackle bedtime solo.
- Take the kids to school on your partner's day.
- Ask "What can I do to make your day better today?"

Acts of Service Date Ideas:
- Cook dinner together.
- Finish a DIY project together.
- Stay in and have a massage night, focused on your partner.
- Surprise your partner at work with an impromptu lunch date.

Acts of Service Gift Ideas:
- Breakfast in bed
- Taking all the laundry (including bedspreads) to the dry cleaner
- Steam cleaning the carpets
- Coupon books filled with Acts of Service coupons
- A robotic vacuum

Acts of Service What to Avoid:
- **Breaking promises**
  If you have committed to doing something for your partner, be sure to follow through. Your acts are especially meaningful, and if you fail to follow through, your partner will be extra disappointed.
- **Overcommitting to tasks**
  As a general rule in life, you should under-promise and over-deliver. This is even more true when you're communicating

with someone whose love language is Acts of Service. Your actions are meaningful to your partner, so be sure to only commit to the things you can do and do well.

◆ **Not doing your part around the house**

Your partner feels loved by you when you do things around the house. When you don't do your part, the opposite is true. Your partner doesn't feel loved by you. Put in an intentional effort to help around the home to show your partner you're thinking of them.

◆ **Letting your partners' actions go unacknowledged**

Your partner uses actions to show their love because that's what is most meaningful to them. If you don't acknowledge when they have done something for you, it feels like you are dismissing their love.

QUALITY TIME

Quality Time means spending uninterrupted, intentional time together as a couple. Date night will be especially meaningful for someone with this primary love language. But it doesn't have to be a scheduled event; the time spent together connecting–not the activity–is most important.

Examples of Quality Time:

◆ Plan a date night.
◆ Take a walk together.
◆ Play a board game.
◆ Discuss your goals and how you can achieve them together.
◆ Slow dance in the living room.
◆ Cheer on your favorite team together.
◆ Have a picnic in the park.
◆ Go for a road trip.
◆ Visit a farmer's market and go home and cook together.
◆ Watch the sunset or sunrise.
◆ Recreate your first date.
◆ Buy tickets for a movie or play they've been wanting to see.
◆ Book a sitter so you can have some alone time.
◆ Have a deep conversation with eye contact and undivided attention.

Quality Time Date Ideas:

- Camp under the stars.
- Go hiking.
- Attend an art festival or concert.
- Visit a museum.
- Try something new, like a workout class.
- Enjoy a glass of wine and good conversation at a wine bar.

Quality Time Gift Ideas:

- Gift certificate to their favorite restaurant
- Board games or puzzles you can do together
- Reservation for two at a Bed and Breakfast
- Tickets to see their favorite team play

Quality Time What to Avoid:

- **Using your phone during quality time**

  Your partner wants your undivided attention. Quality time is broken when there are distractions. I recently saw a video of Simon Sinek (of *Start With Why* fame) giving a speech. He asked the audience how their perception of his attention changed when he picked up his phone. It wasn't buzzing; he wasn't looking at it. He was simply holding it. He asked and answered, "Do you feel like you are the most important thing to me right now? No, you don't. That is the association."[46] Don't give your partner (who feels most loved by you with quality time) the impression that your phone is more important to you than they are.

- **Letting too much time pass between date nights**

  Your partner needs this dedicated time to feel loved by you. Avoid droughts to keep them feeling connected with you.

- **Spending more time in group settings instead of as a couple**

  Your partner loves spending time with you in any capacity, but group settings are not a replacement for time as a couple. Make sure that you plan intentional time for the two of you in addition to family time and time with friends.

WORDS OF AFFIRMATION

Someone whose primary love language is Words of Affirmation needs to hear loving, appreciative words. Telling this person what you love about them, how grateful you are for them, or complimenting them will make them feel most loved.

Examples of Words of Affirmation:

- Have flowers delivered with a note.
- Leave a loving sticky note on the bathroom mirror, coffee maker, and so on, where your partner will find it in the morning.
- Purchase a greeting card with a thoughtful message.
- Send a text message with love song lyrics.
- Share your three favorite things about them with them.
- Tell someone else in front of them how proud you are of them or how much you appreciate them.
- Post a photo of the two of you on social media with a caption of gratitude, love, acknowledgment, appreciation, and so forth.
- Tell your partner why you're thankful that they're in your life.
- Send a "Thinking of you" text.
- Remind your partner of a sweet memory and how it made you feel.
- Say "I love you," "Thank you," "I appreciate you," "My life is better because you're in it," and so on.

Words of Affirmation Date Ideas:

- Attend a karaoke night where you sing songs that represent your feelings.
- Create a love note or memory scavenger hunt.
- Host a vow renewal.
- Share a dinner date where you discuss your dreams and make a plan to achieve them together.

Words of Affirmation Gift Ideas:

- A greeting card with the perfect heartfelt message
- Journal with your love story
- Scrapbook of your love story
- An original poem

Words of Affirmation What to Avoid:

- **Offering insincere or exaggerated compliments**
  Affirm your partner authentically. Let them know the things about them that you most admire and love, but don't sugarcoat or fib. These affirmations should both *be* genuine and *feel* genuine to your partner.

◆ **Using hurtful language or being verbally abusive**
Because your words hold so much power for someone with this love language, unkind words wield the same power. Hold your tongue. Your partner will internalize your cruel comments and have a challenging time forgetting them.

◆ **Being overly critical**
Your partner is so in tune with and responsive to your feedback that your criticism is especially affective. Be mindful of how frequently you are giving corrective feedback, and be sure that when you do, it's necessary.

RECEIVING GIFTS

For some people, receiving meaningful gifts resonates the most deeply. The gifts don't need to be expensive, just thoughtful! Picking up your partner's favorite treat at the grocery store, sending them their favorite flowers just because, or surprising them with that gadget they mentioned wanting in passing, all these things make this person feel seen and loved by you.

Examples of Receiving Gifts:
◆ Get a gift certificate for their favorite restaurant and encourage them to have a night out with friends.
◆ Send them a surprise gift at work.
◆ Make a mixtape and explain why you chose each song.
◆ Create a photobook or scrapbook of memories together.
◆ Have cookies delivered randomly.
◆ When traveling alone, bring back a souvenir for your partner.
◆ Find something to add to their collection and wrap it up for a surprise.
◆ Grab a unique present to celebrate an obscure holiday (e.g., tortilla warmer for Taco Tuesday).
◆ Purchase tickets to a show, concert, or game they'd love to attend.
◆ Sign them up for a class they've been wanting to take.

Receiving Gifts Date Ideas:
◆ Surprise them with a shopping spree at their favorite store.

- Visit an art gallery where you purchase a piece of art you both love.
- Enjoy a painting night together where you give each other your finished projects.
- Shop for items at a unique gift shop or antique store where your partner may find something they love.

Receiving Gifts Gift Ideas:

- Gift certificate to a favorite restaurant or store
- T-shirt or sweatshirt for their favorite team or TV show
- A new video game
- Something they've been wanting for a while

Receiving Gifts What to Avoid:

- **Forgetting special events**

  For someone with a primary love language of Receiving Gifts, they look forward to the thoughtful gifts they'll receive for special events. Forgetting about these is especially disappointing for someone with this love language. Make sure they're on your calendar, with reminders set up and a plan in place.

- **Giving impersonal gifts**

  It's the thought that counts here more than anything! Don't give this person a generic gift card, a candle (unless they really love them), or anything else you'd purchase for someone you barely know. This gift should be something that shows you know your partner and their interests on a deeper level.

PHYSICAL TOUCH

The final love language is Physical Touch. Some people need to be held and touched by their partners to feel loved. While this can certainly be sexual intercourse, it can also be holding hands, rubbing their shoulders, or a kiss to greet them when they get home from work.

Examples of Physical Touch:

- Cuddle your partner.
- Give a hug, just because.
- Kiss your partner hello and goodbye.

- Give a high five to celebrate a win.
- Make out like teenagers.
- Check your partner out when you know they're watching.
- Make love.
- Dance with your partner.
- Run your fingers through their hair.
- Touch the small of their back when you walk by.
- Put your arm around them when you're sitting next to them.
- Extend foreplay.
- Hold their hand in the car.
- Give your partner a foot rub.
- Tickle your partner.
- Give a light kiss.

Physical Touch Date Ideas:
- Walk through the park, holding hands.
- Enjoy a spa date or hangout in your hot tub.
- Take a couple's yoga class where you work on poses together.
- Spend a night at home and play a sexy game.

Physical Touch Gift Ideas:
- Massage oil
- A new dress or shirt and a promise of a night out dancing
- Gift certificate for a couple's massage

Physical Touch What to Avoid:
- **Withholding physical affection, especially as a form of control**

  Your touch means so much to your partner that when it is withheld, they feel unloved by you. Don't use your touch (equal in their mind to your love) as a weapon. You're allowed to be upset with your partner when warranted, but you are not allowed to be mean.

- **Neglecting your partner**

  Neglect is not excusable in any relationship, but it's especially painful for someone with this love language. Touch is so meaningful to someone with a love language of Physical

Touch that when it's withheld, it sends the opposite message: You are not loved.

◆ **Using threats or abusive behavior**

While I never advocate for these activities, it's especially important not to do these to someone with this primary love language. For them, when touch is used with malice, it's even more impactful. Mean touch is the quickest way to make this person feel disrespected and unsupported by you.

BRIDGING THE GAP BETWEEN LOVE LANGUAGES

If you and your partner aren't aligned with your love languages, it doesn't mean your relationship is doomed. In fact, when ranking our love languages, my primary love language is Kevin's lowest, and his highest is my lowest. And yet, we have a relationship in which we both consistently feel loved, because we learned about the Five Love Languages.

Naturally, you speak the love language that is most natural and meaningful to you. When your partner has the same love language, it is received with the full impact it was intended, and the relationship has been nurtured. But for many of us, our partners don't have the same love language. Our relationships take more intentionality to nurture.

Kevin's love language doesn't come naturally to me. In fact, it doesn't even make sense to me. He's an Acts of Service guy, and it just doesn't compute in my brain. I do the dishes because they're dirty, not because I love you (although I do). My Words of Affirmation brain needs to ensure that was directly communicated with the English language. In fact, I'm almost evenly balanced between Words of Affirmation and Quality Time. (Remember when I wanted Kevin to visit, even if it was a quick visit?) Words of Affirmation don't come easily to him. He wants to make sure his words around love are perfectly articulated and meaningful. What he doesn't understand is that any words of affirmation are perfect and meaningful to me when they come from him.

Though you may not understand why your partner's love language is impactful to them, you can still speak it. It likely will not come naturally to you, so be intentional. Put a reminder somewhere you will see it daily and honor that commitment by finding a way to speak their love language every single day. I like to set a recurring reminder on my phone stating, "Have you spoken Kevin's love language today?" If I haven't, it's the nudge I need!

ADDITIONAL RESOURCES

If my descriptions weren't enough or you're waffling between a few love languages, I highly recommend going straight to the source to learn more! Dr. Gary Chapman's book, *The 5 Love Languages: The Secret to Love That Lasts*, is an incredible resource. Or you can head to 5lovelanguages.com and take the online quiz. Once you and your partner each have your results, sit down for some uninterrupted time and share your ranking of love languages and examples of things your partner can do to make you feel most loved.

Activity: Discuss Your Love Languages

1. Rank the Five Love Languages from most meaningful to least meaningful. Brainstorm at least three ways that your partner can speak your primary love language.
2. Have your partner do the same.
3. Discuss your love languages with each other. Ask in-depth questions such as, "When was a time you felt truly loved by me? What did I do that made you feel that way?" and "When is a time you haven't felt appreciated or loved by me? What would have made you feel loved instead?" Ask clarifying questions to really understand what your partner needs and how they feel.
4. Set a reminder to speak your partner's love language every day.

The Reminder You Didn't Know You Needed

> *"Don't sweat the small stuff, and it's all small stuff."*[47]
> – Richard Carlson, author and psychotherapist

Being a stepparent and second wife is far more challenging than I anticipated. Call me naive, but I didn't realize I would face added complexities in a stepfamily that those in a nuclear family don't face. I didn't know I'd have such strong opinions on my spouse's ex-wife, how their child should be raised, and what co-parenting should mean for us. I also failed to realize that not only were those opinions ignorant and shortsighted, but they were also largely unwelcome.

I began to understand something very significant. My role in this stepfamily is as a wife first and a stepmom second.

Remember Jenna Korf, who told us we should be talking to our partner like they're the person we love most in this world? The *Skirts at War* author has another great reminder for us. I know I've struggled with this battle, and so many stepmoms I've worked with have as well.

Korf once asked me, "Is it more important for us to have a happy, healthy marriage, or is it more important that [my partner] raise [their] kids the way I believe they should be raised?"

Pretty powerful, isn't it?

Many stepmoms don't want to have to make a choice. They want both: to be right and to be happy. The odds are stacked against you in a stepcouple relationship, so you must be determined to do everything you can to strengthen your couple bond and to beat the odds. One of the best ways you can do that is to focus first on your relationship, and less on your opinions of your partner's ex, their child, and their co-parenting.

Early in our relationship, before we had our son together, I was a childless stepmom whose spouse has joint custody. Half of the time, it was just my husband and me. If I hadn't prioritized our marriage, we would have been lost on our "off" days when my stepdaughter was at her mom's home. I know that someday, my stepdaughter is going to fly the coop and go to college, live in her own home, and so on, and I don't want my partner to be a stranger when that day comes. The family cannot determine the marriage; the marriage must set the tone for the family.

My family situation will not look like this forever, but my marriage will. For that reason, I can't allow different parenting styles or any other family disagreements to be prioritized above my desire to have a happy, healthy relationship with Kevin.

Of course, it's okay to be your own person in a relationship: to have your own interests, to disagree on some things, and to have opinions separate from your partner. But those differences should never be the focus. When you choose to focus on what you dislike or what separates you, then you're moving further away from one another instead of closer together as a couple.

If my top priority is a happy, healthy marriage, then it's imperative I don't focus on differences, especially those that are tied to his ex-wife and my stepdaughter, or anything else outside of my control. There will always be disagreements or differences. Choosing to focus on the things we agree on improves my mood, my relationship with my stepdaughter, and my relationship with my husband.

IT'S NOT TOO LATE TO CHANGE YOUR ANSWER

At the end of the day, even if I disagree with Kevin's decisions, I still trust his judgment. I married him because I think he's an intelligent, compassionate, and logical person whose heart is always in the right place. If I felt truly disrespected, I'd feel comfortable voicing those feelings, and my husband would definitely correct his course. But when it comes to less offensive parenting style differences, I will make a conscious effort to prioritize my marriage instead.

You chose your partner for a reason. Despite all the complications, stressors—dare I say, baggage?—they came with. You trust them, or else you wouldn't be with them. You wouldn't be reading this book and doing everything in your power to make it. Trust that you chose someone who will make educated decisions, even if you disagree with those choices.

HELPFUL TIPS FOR CHOOSING YOUR RELATIONSHIP

- ◆ Walk away when you disagree.
  If your partner is disciplining (or choosing not to) in a way you disagree with, choose to walk away from the situation. Staying in an uncomfortable situation that affects your perspective of your partner is unproductive at best, and counterproductive at worst. Ignorance is sometimes bliss. Remove yourself from uncomfortable and triggering situations so they don't pile up and affect your views of your partner.

- ◆ Ask yourself if this truly matters.
  Remember our discussion on choosing your battles? Is this a battle worth choosing? Will this matter in five years? Is this disagreement more important than a happy, healthy marriage?

◆ Find something you can control.

If you're feeling helpless in your home, focus on what is within your control. Get a date night on the calendar, cook dinner, or take up gardening. Taking back control over something else helps in all areas.

◆ Remember to do more of the things that make you, you.

By now, you know that stepmomming is what you do, it's not who you are. This is important! Don't forget to do the things that make you, *you*.

If you loved painting before you became a stepmom, pick up your brushes and a fresh canvas. If you miss your girlfriends, call them up for a girls' night out. It's not sustainable for this role to become your whole identity. So, do the things you love–the things that breathe life into you.

This works twofold for choosing your partner over your parenting style preferences:

1. When you feel more like yourself, you're less resentful of your partner. Having a clearer mind and better mood carries over into everyday life. It's easier to choose your battles, you're less likely to get triggered, and if you do become triggered, you're less likely to let resentment fester.
2. You can opt for a preferred activity instead of staying stuck in a frustrating situation with your partner.

A couple of years ago, I had a client whose partner took his daughter to Target every single Wednesday on his midweek visitation. My client was so frustrated at the excess: the spending and the spoiling. Every time Wednesday rolled around, her anxiety shot through the roof, knowing she'd be triggered all over again that evening. That is, until Wednesday became the perfect evening for her to spend with her own daughter and granddaughter. She was distracted from her partner's "poor parenting" by filling her own cup: Win-win!

Rediscover your passions, hobbies, and loved ones that make you feel like you again. It's important that stepmomming doesn't consume your entire life. Regaining these joys in your life will enable some of the frustrations to roll off your back much easier. And when all else fails, ask yourself the most important question you can ask in a second marriage:

Is it more important for us to have a happy, healthy marriage or is it more important that [my partner] raise [their] kids the way I believe they should be raised?

—Jenna Korf, Certified Stepfamily Coach

A happy, healthy marriage is far more important to me long term than bedtime, chores, or being right. I choose us every single time. I am a wife first, and a stepmom second.

Activity: Reframe Your Frustration

The next time you find yourself frustrated with your partner's parenting choices, ask yourself, "Is it more important for us to have a happy, healthy relationship, or is it more important that my partner raise their kids the way I believe they should be raised?"

Habits for a Healthy Relationship

"The single biggest problem in communication is the illusion that it has taken place."[48]

– George Bernard Shaw, playwright and critic

This book has covered several subtopics of healthy relationships already, and next it covers pitfalls to avoid. If it's starting to feel like this is a marriage book, that's because it kind of is. Without your romantic relationship, you don't have a stepfamily. Every other relationship in this dynamic is dependent on the one you share with your partner.

Beyond the larger concepts I've already introduced, I want to ensure that you're implementing regular habits to foster your bond.

The first big habit I want you to regularly do is to designate a connection ritual that you and your partner can do daily. I want this to supersede custodial time, so you'll still do this connection activity whether your stepchildren are in your home or not.

One of the biggest complaints I hear from stepmoms is that they feel like they lose their partner when their stepchildren are in their home. It's one thing to say that your marriage is a priority, but it's another thing entirely to show it. By now, you know all the feelings and the guilt behind your partner's actions and decisions. But empathizing with their perspective doesn't change the fact that you deserve to feel prioritized and loved 24/7 as well.

Designating a time for the two of you to connect each and every single day will validate you as the stepmom, send a positive message to the children about healthy relationships, and strengthen your partnership. This doesn't need to be a significantly long period of time, but it should be quality time spent together. (See how it's all tying together? It's almost like I wrote this book in an intentional order.)

Kevin and I really enjoy going for a walk each day. We get our bodies moving, get some Vitamin D, and get to hold hands and talk to each other away from work, home, and other responsibilities. It's not often a long walk; even 20 minutes helps us connect and recenter as a couple each day. That daily time together isn't a big investment for Kevin, but it makes me feel like the most special person in his life.

If going for a walk isn't your speed (pun intended), maybe you prefer doing one of these activities together:

- Drinking your coffee in the morning
- Doing the *New York Times* crossword puzzle
- Watching a TV series, one episode per day
- Enjoying a night cap or mocktail
- Playing your favorite video game
- Hitting up the gym

This time spent together daily will ensure that you stay connected and aligned as a couple. The more loved you feel, the more confident you are, and the better you show up in all your roles and relationships.

The second habit I want you two to develop is meeting regularly. (I prefer Sunday or Monday to start the week off right.) Plan to spend time weekly to discuss what's going well, and what could be going better. These regular check-ins help you to get ahead of any potential emotional landmines. By discussing your struggles or triggers early and often, you'll feel more like a team, reduce resentment, and see the progress made toward your goals.

Set aside recurring time on your calendars to have these conversations. Start with appreciation for what's going well. Peaceful times don't happen by chance, so catalog what's working to ensure it *keeps* working. Then, take turns and address what you'd like to see improved. Use your feelings and words and let your partner know what you need in return.

For example, if I was feeling triggered by the clutter and mess around the house, I would say, "Babe, I'm feeling overwhelmed by the clutter in the home. I could really use some help picking up the house this week." Notice I've used "I" statements and communicated directly. I'm not beating around the bush. I'm not telling my partner what they've done wrong. I'm expressing my feelings and needs.

Combining these two habits will give you and your partner a framework for success. You'll be regularly strengthening your relationship through daily bonding, and weekly positive reinforcement and realignment.

Activity: Implement Connection Activities
Discuss these habits with your partner and decide on:

1. Your daily connection activity and time
2. Your weekly meeting time

Relationship Pitfalls to Avoid

> *"In healthy relationships, both partners are more focused on solving the problem than assigning blame."*
>
> – Unknown

I've said it before, and I'll likely say it a dozen times more: Your relationship is the foundation of the family. It deserves prioritization and requires nourishment. To maintain an unshakable relationship, you'll want to avoid these common pitfalls.

PITFALL #1: KEEPING SCORE IN YOUR RELATIONSHIP
This will probably sound obvious to some of you, but it's important not to keep score. It's a good rule for life in general … unless you're a professional athlete or play an intramural sport. When it comes to the relationship with your partner, however, keeping score will

drive you bonkers at best, and completely demolish your relationship at worst. The truth is, relationships in blended families already start at a disadvantage compared to first marriages, due to all their added complexities. It's imperative that you stop adding numbers and applying arbitrary meaning to little moments.

Scorekeeping can look like keeping track of who's performing which surface-level activities like chores, childcare, and who picks up the tab at dinner. It can also apply to deeper-level connections, like which partner initiates sex. Some of us keep score of how much time is spent alone versus together, or which partner's friends and family members we've seen more often. If you feel like you are sacrificing for your relationship, and that things aren't reciprocal, you'll be more likely to want to keep score.

But here's the trouble. Scorekeeping sets you up to believe in all-or-nothing concepts (I always, You never... and so on). You could find you're quick to respond in defense mode when you keep score. If your partner expresses a complaint, your arsenal will be loaded with your latest contribution and their score deficit, ready for your rebuttal. This defensiveness shuts down the conversation–or worse, escalates it into a conflict. As a result, you won't hear your partner's concern and request, and they won't hear yours. You two will become even more disconnected.

With this type of thinking and behavior, you'll feel misunderstood, resentful, and frustrated. It's a "me"-centered way of operating, but your relationship needs to be a mutual space. Scorekeeping elevates one of you out of your shared space. If your score is up, then your partner's score is down, and neither of you can win. Your relationship certainly isn't winning.

If you find yourself stuck in score-keeping or negative thinking, there are ways to course correct. Make it a goal to rebuttal each "tally" with something positive your partner has done. For example, if you find you're constantly emptying the clean dishwasher, consider another task they do regularly, like taking the trash to the curb.

Furthermore, recognize that relationships aren't 50/50 all the time. Work, family stress, financial pressure, or any other number of stressors could be causing one of you to not be able to contribute exactly equally at any given moment. Scorekeeping doesn't allow for this kind of natural fluctuation in schedules and capacity. Give yourself and your partner grace, knowing you can pick up each other's slack as needed.

Finally, remember my biggest rule for stepmoms: "If you can't do something graciously, don't do it." Only give in ways you can give without expectation. If doing the dishes one more time is going to make you feel resentful and try to count the number of times you've done the dishes recently, instead opt for telling your partner, "Hey babe, I would really appreciate it if you could do the dishes tonight." Instead of folding another load of clothes, you might mention, "Honey, I think it's really sexy when you do the kids' laundry. You're such a good parent."

Activity: Survey Your Partner's Contributions

If you find yourself scorekeeping, make a list of everything your partner has done for you, the children, or the household in the last week. Appreciate their contributions, even if they feel unequal to yours.

If you're still resentful and feeling a tendency to score keep, step away from tasks that feel especially draining and are directly contributing to the lack of reciprocity.

PITFALL #2: THINKING IT'S ME VERSUS YOU, INSTEAD OF US VERSUS THE ISSUE

Similar in nature and severity to scorekeeping is a mindset that when conflict arises, it's me versus you. Thinking that your partner is the enemy, and you need to defeat them to win. This is a massive pitfall many stepcouples fall into. You two need to be on the same team. It should always be us versus the issue, not me versus you.

I've been working with a client for a few years, while her partner works to finalize his divorce, initiated by his ex over a year before he met my client. His ex has dragged on the proceedings for years. My client has become, rightfully so, impatient and frustrated with the process. But (as I'm sure you can relate), he happens to be the perfect guy otherwise. Don't you hate it when they do that?

I could fill an entire chapter with the manipulation and stalling tactics this woman has used to drag out their divorce. Not because she wants to be married to him or because she's mad he's dating someone new–because she can't afford the lifestyle she's accustomed to, without him. As a result, one of the very first skills that I had to help my client develop is a mindset of "us versus the issue." It would have been so easy to pin every delay on him. To blame him for the loss of time, money, and energy, as a result of his prolonged divorce proceedings. But she doesn't blame him; she works alongside him to tackle the issue at hand, as a team.

You are allowed to be frustrated. Your first response doesn't have to be the mature one. You're completely entitled to your reactions to the actions and words of others. But don't let anyone or anything divide you and your partner from the strong team you are. Don't let them win. You're stronger than that. You deserve better than that.

Activity: Reframe Your Mindset

Make "us versus the issue" your new mantra! You and your partner are a team, so remind yourself of that as often as you need to in order to reframe your mindset.

PITFALL #3: NOT MAKING TIME TO CONNECT AS A COUPLE

Life is busy. But if you aren't taking intentional time to strengthen your bond, you're setting your relationship up to fail. I'm sorry if that sounds dramatic or intense, especially after validating how busy life can get, but it's true. Every relationship needs nurturing, but those like ours, with its added stressors and complexities, requires even more intentional effort.

Regularly make time to check in with each other. Go on dates. Be intimate. Don't put off important conversations. Prioritize your connection like the future of your relationship depends on it.

Activity: Schedule Date Night

Get a date night on the calendar!

Communicating Through Conflict and Finding Compromise

> *"Conflict is not the opposite of love. It's an opportunity to go deeper into understanding of your partner and create a relationship that is more connected and more loving."*[49]
> – Ted Riter, rabbi, coach, mentor, and teacher of intimacy and transformation

Conflict often arises as a result of unmet expectations. When you have expectations of how an event should go, how your stepchildren should behave, or how your partner should show their love for you, and those expectations aren't met, a divide has been created. The divide must be bridged; conflict must be repaired.

Easier said than done, right? Communicating about conflict, when you're feeling triggered, disappointed, or upset, might feel impossible without yelling or saying something unkind. When we're in a heightened state, it can be incredibly challenging to sort through our emotions and have a level-headed, productive conversation. This becomes even more complicated in a blended family when your partner might also be in an emotional or defensive state.

When your partner is wrapped up in their own emotions, especially if one of their primary core values is triggered, they might be unable to have a constructive, respectful conversation with you. In fact, what they might be hearing is actually the opposite of what you're communicating, and the opposite of your intentions. Their own biases and insecurities can impede healthy communication.

Let's look at an example. My client, Rachel, was blending families with her new husband, Patrick. She brought three kids to the marriage, and he brought two. His youngest had an especially difficult time adjusting to life in a blended family. She acted out, made life difficult on her siblings, and challenged her stepmom's patience. When Rachel brought this up to Patrick in a collaborative way with kind words and "I" statements, Patrick's walls instantly rose. Instead of hearing, "How can we help your daughter adjust and help our whole family feel more comfortable?" he heard, "Your daughter is a brat, and we're all ganging up on her." He couldn't hear his wife's true intentions, because of his insecurities about his divorce. He worried that he chose his own happiness over his children's, and that he ruined their lives in the process.

Perhaps you're nodding along with this example because you have a similar one of your own. Emotions run high in a blended family. When one or both of you is feeling triggered, it's not the right time to have the conversation. The conversation will only continue to escalate, and there will likely be no positive outcome or resolution. Take time to process your own reactions, recenter, and assume positive intent from your partner. Remember: You're on the same team. Then, when you're ready, try the conversation again.

TIPS TO MITIGATE A DEFENSIVE RESPONSE

Defensiveness is unfortunately fairly common in stepcouples. Our relationships are so personal that when something doesn't go the way we want it to, we take that feedback personally. And yet, we're all trying as hard as we possibly can. It feels like a personal failure, and we become defensive.

Defensiveness is toxic in relationships. At its core, defensiveness is a way to blame your partner. When you get defensive, you're essentially saying, "I'm not the problem. You are." And, of course, that's not helpful or kind. You're not going to see a positive quick resolution after telling your partner they're the problem.

To mitigate the chance your partner feels attacked–and subsequently, defensive–be conscientious about your approach. Be intentional with your timing. Word your concerns carefully and considerately. Assume positive intent and seek to understand when you can't find the positive intent. Then, work together to find a satisfactory solution for both of you.

TIP #1: ASK WHEN IT WOULD BE A GOOD TIME FOR A DISCUSSION

One of the biggest mistakes I made in my early days as a stepmom learning how to communicate effectively was rushing into conversations. I was impatient and needed resolution NOW. Rushing the conversation never worked well, however. Your partner might be distracted, harboring negative feelings from something else going on, or otherwise not ready to have the conversation with you.

Let them know there's something you'd like to discuss and ask when a good time would be to meet. This gives your partner time to collect their thoughts, sort out whatever else may be distracting them, and give you their undivided attention.

TIP #2: OPEN WITH A COMPLIMENT

When you can open the conversation with a related, genuine compliment, it helps break down the defensive walls before they're erected. You'll want to anticipate your partner's sensitivity to the topic before initiating the conversation. If you're going to bring up a desire for house rules, but you worry your partner will be resistant to structure out of a fear of pushing their children away, you might start by saying, "Babe, I think you're such a great parent. It's obvious to me how much your children respect and enjoy being with you."

Make sure this compliment is authentic. You should never lie to your partner. They'll see through it, and it will cause them to feel defensive from the onset. It's definitely not a good start to the conversation. I also want to be sure the compliment is related. If you open that same conversation about house rules with, "Honey, you are such a hard worker. I appreciate how hard you work for our family," they'll appreciate the compliment but become skeptical later when they realize the compliment seemed to just be blowing smoke up their bum.

TIP #3: USE "I" STATEMENTS

As you discuss with your partner, describe your experience from your perspective. Instead of saying, "You don't enforce rules," try stating, "I feel frustrated and overwhelmed when dirty dishes are left in the sink, and I would feel protected and respected if there was a list of house rules and expectations for everyone in our home." You're discussing your experience and the feelings you have when your request isn't honored. You're giving your partner the steps to take to protect you, without accusing or reprimanding them.

Notice how I phrased my statement. I said, "I feel frustrated and overwhelmed when dirty dishes are left in the sink, and I would feel protected and respected if there was a list of house rules and expectations for everyone in our home," I did not say, "When your kids leave dirty dishes in the sink" or "When you don't ask your kids to wash their dishes." I left my phrasing entirely focused on my experience, so my partner doesn't get distracted by an urge to defend their children or themselves.

TIP #4: AVOID GENERALIZATIONS

When you're exasperated because an issue has recurred enough times, you might be tempted to say things like, "The kids *always* leave dirty dishes in the sink" and "You *never* ask them to clean up!" What these generalized statements do, however, is leave our partner wanting to find the one exception to the rule, instead of hearing what you're actually trying to say, which is that you need help and want to feel at home in your home: "That's not true! Three Tuesdays ago, I asked them to load the dishwasher!" Avoid using generalized sweeping statements.

TIP #5: ASK QUESTIONS TO UNDERSTAND THEIR EXPERIENCE AND TO VALIDATE IT

One of the very best ways to mitigate defensiveness and work together as a team is to ask your partner questions to understand their perspective. Why are they acting the way they are? What motivates them? What do they need in this situation?

We can assume their motivation isn't to hurt you or make you feel anything negative ever. That's simply an unfortunate unintentional byproduct of their actions. Seeking to understand their perspective will help you move forward as a united team. Once you have the answers to these questions, not only will your partner feel less defensive and more validated, you'll also be better equipped to move forward and find a compromise.

TIP #6: IF NECESSARY, PAUSE THE CONVERSATION SO YOU CAN EACH IDENTIFY YOUR CORE NEEDS AND COME BACK TOGETHER TO FIND A COMPROMISE

When emotions are running high or someone is feeling defensive, it can be nearly impossible to have a productive, healthy conversation. If you find that either (or both) of you is not in a stable place to continue the conversation right now, the very best thing you can do for your relationship is to take a beat and revisit later. Allow your mind to calm, your heart rate to come down, and recenter on your needs.

I used to be so hesitant and resistant to this process. Walking away felt like I failed. Kevin, taking time to recenter himself, triggered my abandonment insecurity. I wanted to fight for our relationship. But the more I fought, the further apart we grew, and the less progress we made. Begrudgingly, I had to admit he was right. Taking time to pause and then come back to the conversation with a clear head and a calm heart truly helped us to have more connected and solution-oriented discussions.

FINDING COMPROMISE

It can be extremely difficult to reach a compromise when it feels like you and your partner are on opposite sides of an issue. The reality is, it's often not black and white. One of my favorite ways to coach couples through challenging conflicts is by diving into each of their perspectives and truly drilling down into their individual core needs. When you can dig into the need behind the stance, you can really understand how to meet both of your needs. A creative solution can almost always be found that enables the needs of both parties to be met, by compromising on related factors. When you find yourself at an impasse with your partner, use this circle exercise tool from Dr. Gottman, an American psychologist specializing in couples therapy shown in Figure 7.1, to help you visualize compromise.[50]

First, begin by taking a piece of scrap paper and drawing two circles: one larger one and a smaller one within that circle. Write your core need in the smaller circle. Then, think about all the factors you could compromise on, and write those in the outer circle. Your partner should do the same on their own paper with their own circles. Work together to find a solution which will enable each of your core needs in the inner circles to be met by using your outer circles as inspiration for a creative compromise.

Let's imagine there's been a disagreement about who's going to wash the dirty dishes. The messy kitchen overwhelms Stepmom, and she feels underappreciated. Her partner agrees that the kids need to pull their weight around the home, but the idea of

3 Steps of the Circle Exercise

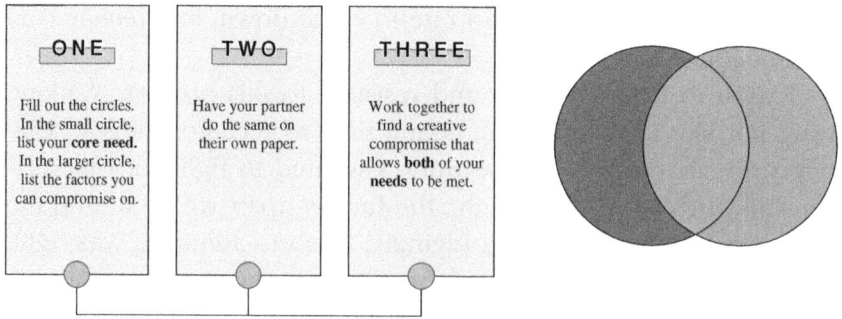

Figure 7.1   The three steps of circle exercise.

Figure 7.2   Circles framework for compromise: stepmom's core need.

asking their children to help triggers guilt and fear. They want to support their partner, but they don't want to do anything that could push their children away.

When Stepmom sits down to work on her circles, she digs to recognize what she really needs. She contemplates what would give her the most peace of mind and mitigate resentment. She decides to write, "I don't want to wake up to a sink full of dirty dishes" in her inner circle, as shown in Figure 7.2.

She then brainstorms various ways to accomplish the goal of an empty sink in the morning. She thinks about the different factors that affect that outcome. Her outer circle, as shown in Figure 7.3, says:

- ◆ The dishes can be washed late at night or early in the morning.
- ◆ The dishes can be hand-washed or in the dishwasher.
- ◆ Paper plates can be used instead of dishes.
- ◆ The dishes can be washed by my partner or my stepchildren.

What matters to her most is that she doesn't wake up to a sink full of dirty dishes. Her ideal solution would be to have her partner remind the children to wash their dishes and hold them accountable. But that triggers her partner, so it isn't the optimal solution. Your compromise needs to work for both of you.

Stepmom's compromise factors

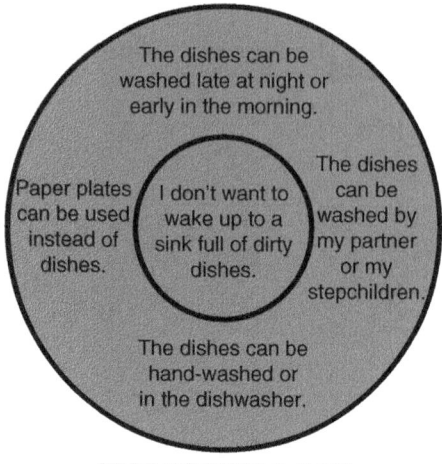

The dishes can be washed late at night or early in the morning.

Paper plates can be used instead of dishes.

I don't want to wake up to a sink full of dirty dishes.

The dishes can be washed by my partner or my stepchildren.

The dishes can be hand-washed or in the dishwasher.

STEPMOMMING.COM

Figure 7.3   Circles framework for compromise: stepmom's compromise factors.

When her partner sits down to work on their circles, their core need feels obvious: "I don't want to nag my kids." They write it in the inner circle, as depicted in Figure 7.4.

As they brainstorm how to compromise, they identify a few ways they can accomplish the goal of eliminating dirty dishes without nagging. Their outer circle, as you'll see in Figure 7.5, includes:

- ◆ I can wash the dishes.
- ◆ We can use a chore chart.
- ◆ We can pay allowance for chores.

Because what matters to them most is that they don't have to nag their children to wash the dishes. Asking once feels perfectly reasonable. Designating chores would feel okay too, especially if the children are paid an allowance upon completion.

When we can break the disconnect down in this way, it makes finding compromise exponentially easier. Take a look at the two core needs, displayed in Figure 7.6: "I don't want to wake up to a sink full of dirty dishes" and "I don't want to nag my kids." We can achieve both things! There are several compromises they might reach, but for the sake of the example, let's pretend they decided

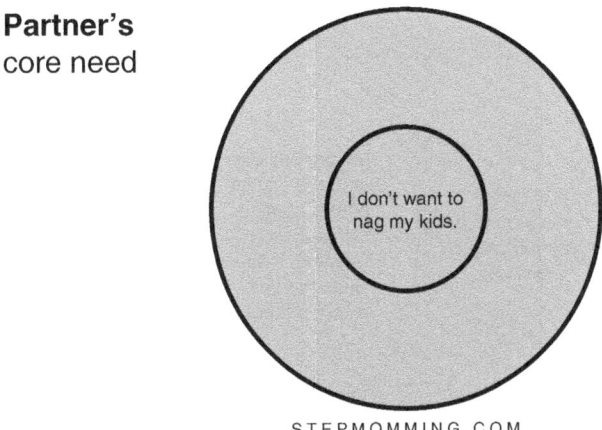

Figure 7.4   Circles framework for compromise: partner's core need.

Figure 7.5   Circles framework for compromise: partner's compromise factors.

on: "My partner will wash the dishes before coming to bed each evening, if the kids haven't washed them." Stepmom wakes up to a clean kitchen, and her partner doesn't have to nag their children. Win-win!

Activity: Use the Circles Framework for Compromise

Think about the last disagreement you had with your partner where it felt like you were on opposing sides with opposite solutions. If you

Compromise

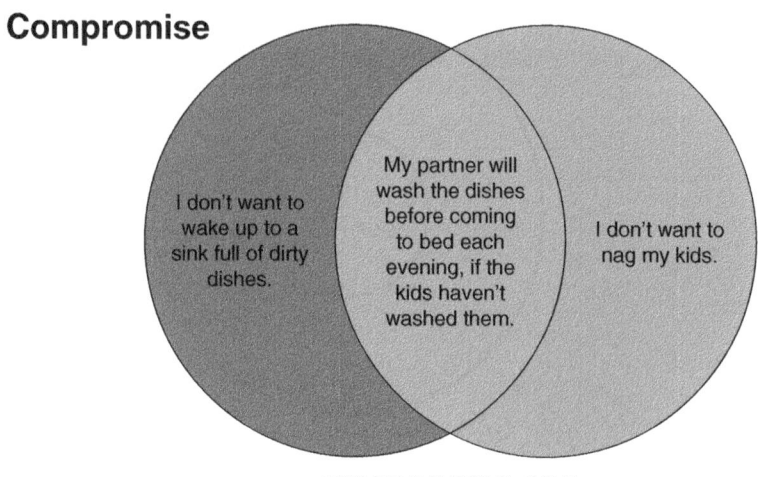

STEPMOMMING.COM

Figure 7.6   Circles framework for compromise: a compromise.

had used the circles framework for compromise, what would your circles have looked like? What do you think your partner's circles would have looked like? How could you have found compromise using this framework?

Saying "I'm Sorry" in Your Partner's Apology Language

> *"Apologizing … means you value your relationship more than your ego."*[51]
>
>   – Mark Matthews, author *of The Power of Apology*

It's no secret that conflict is painful and affects relationships. When someone has done something to hurt or offend you, it immediately creates what authors of *When Sorry Isn't Enough,* Gary Chapman and Jennifer Thomas, the masterminds behind this section, deem "an emotional barrier" between the two of you.[52] Until that emotional barrier has been removed, the relationship hasn't been repaired and cannot continue to grow. Apologizing is how you work to tear down the barrier.

"But What If I Didn't Mean to Hurt Them?"

You should be apologizing even when you didn't mean to hurt or offend your partner. In my work with stepmoms and their partners, I often hear, "But I didn't mean to hurt them, so I don't need to apologize." While I appreciate that you're not intentionally trying to hurt your partner, it doesn't change the fact that, unwillingly and unknowingly, you have hurt them.

Imagine I am walking down a busy street and accidentally bump into someone carrying a hot cup of coffee that spills all over the stranger. I'm not going to choose not to apologize because it was an accident. Of course, it was an accident. But that doesn't change the fact that her gorgeous coat is ruined, and her coffee cup is empty. I am sorry to have disrupted her day like that, to have inconvenienced and hurt her. So, I apologize, even though there was no malicious or unkind intention.

The same is true in our romantic relationship and family. If I give Kevin feedback on his parenting choices that I think is productive and important for the future of our family, but he hears something that makes him feel like I don't trust him to make good decisions, I've unintentionally hurt and offended my husband. I need to repair our relationship. I need to apologize and reset my intentions, even though I never meant to hurt him.

But unless you're apologizing effectively, it will not land correctly. You must be apologizing in your partner's preferred apology language. Just like we can all feel love differently, there are a variety of different styles of apologies too. To repair relationships and remove barriers created from offenses, we need to hear apologies in our preferred language. These are the apologies that are most meaningful and effective. They resonate with us the deepest. Until it's in our preferred language, we can't truly internalize your attempt to repair our relationship.

Before I discovered the apology languages, I would tell Kevin after a disagreement, "I just really need an apology to move forward from this." Exasperated, he would say, "I have apologized!" I didn't understand why we were going round and round when clearly he hadn't apologized yet … right? Wrong. Kevin had been apologizing in his preferred apology language, but I couldn't recognize it because it wasn't *my* preferred apology language.

If this sounds familiar, this discussion is for you, friend!

Effective apologies connect and repair relationships. Mastering your partner's apology language will build trust and strengthen your bond. It is a skill you will repeatedly use with your partner, but it's also a crucial skill in maintaining other relationships. The five apology languages are: Expressing Regret, Accepting Responsibility, Making Restitution, Genuinely Repenting, and Requesting Forgiveness. Let's go deeper on each one, as explained in Chapman and Thomas's book, *When Sorry Isn't Enough.*[52]

EXPRESSING REGRET

"I'm sorry."

Someone who has a preferred apology language of Expressing Regret will absolutely recognize if your attempt to repair does not contain the two critical words: "I'm sorry." They need to hear that you regret hurting them. If your attempt to repair doesn't include a sincere emotional plea, it will not resonate.

You should be expressing to this person your shame and/or pain knowing that you have hurt them. Express regret for how you have treated them and the pain you have caused them. Hearing this emotional plea will enable them to internalize and acknowledge your apology.

Example

"I know I caused you deep pain, and that weighs heavily on me. I am truly sorry for my actions."

ACCEPTING RESPONSIBILITY

"I was wrong."

The language of Accepting Responsibility is all about owning your actions. The offended person doesn't want to hear your excuses;

they want you to acknowledge what you've done wrong and accept responsibility for those actions.

Accepting responsibility is hard for some. Reluctance to admit fault often stems from a need to protect our self-image. An immature person will want to rationalize and make excuses for their behavior. But mature people can accept how their actions–even if unintentional–were wrong and hurt someone else. They're not afraid to recognize their own shortcomings or failures. So, if your partner's primary apology language is Accept Responsibility, you must put aside your ego and admit fault to resolve the conflict and mend the relationship.

Example

"I recognize that my actions were wrong. There's no excuse for my actions–plain and simple, they were selfish and unacceptable."

MAKING RESTITUTION

"How can I make it right?"

Simply saying, "It wasn't right for me to treat you that way," isn't enough for someone with a primary apology language of Making Restitution. They need to hear you express a genuine desire to rectify the situation. They want to know you're willing to put in the work to fix what you have done. Without taking steps to repair the damage, they may struggle to believe that your apology is heartfelt.

To take it a step farther, the impact is significantly greater when it aligns with the other person's primary love language. When you make your repair attempt more personal, it's naturally more effective. Your partner will recognize and appreciate the intentionality. It will expedite the attempt to repair trust and heal the relationship.

Example

"How can I make things right after what I've done?"

GENUINELY REPENTING

"I want to change."

Unless you are truly sorry, any attempt to repair and apologize to someone whose primary apology language is Genuinely Repenting may not be received. When your partner has been hurt, they want to know that you intend to change. They want to be sure you're not going to continue doing the same things and hurting them repeatedly.

To genuinely repent, you must directly communicate to your partner with an intent to change. Without genuine repentance, your partner may be unable to hear and accept your apology.

Example

"I understand that my actions hurt you deeply, and I'm determined not to let that happen again. I'm willing to hear any thoughts you have on how I can change and grow."

REQUESTING FORGIVENESS

"Can you find it in your heart …"

For some people, an apology without a request for forgiveness would be incomplete and unfulfilling. They need to know that you care deeply about repairing and restoring the relationship. They need the opportunity to forgive you for your actions, and without that opportunity, the attempt to repair your relationship will be unsuccessful.

When you request forgiveness, you show that you're prepared to leave the future of the relationship entirely in the hands of the person you've hurt. With an apology language of Requesting Forgiveness, your partner needs the power to accept an apology.

Example

"I deeply regret the pain I caused you and fully understand if you choose to cut ties with me. Still, I want to express how truly sorry I am and hope that forgiveness might be possible in time."

PUTTING IT INTO PRACTICE

I want you to take some time to rank these five apology languages from one to five, based on how meaningful they are to you. What matters most to you in an apology? Which of these five methods really resonated with you? Which seemed the most heartfelt and effective? Answering these questions will guide your rankings. But if you still need some help, head to 5lovelanguages.com and complete the Apology Languages quiz!

Once you've identified which languages are most important to you, have a discussion with your partner about what you need in an apology and why it's particularly effective for you. During conflict, if you aren't getting the type of apology you need, use this new vernacular to express to your partner exactly what you're needing. Try something like, "Babe, I know it feels like we're spinning our wheels right now. What I really need from you right now is Genuine Repentance. I need to trust you know what you did is wrong, and you won't continue this hurtful behavior." This equips your partner with the tools and information to more successfully repair the relationship and remove barriers created by conflict.

Understanding our different apology languages and what we each needed in a repair attempt dramatically changed my relationship. I genuinely hope this has the same positive impact on your relationship when conflict inevitably occurs.

Activity: Discuss Your Apology Languages

1. Rank the Five Apology Languages from most meaningful to least meaningful.
2. Have your partner do the same!
3. Discuss your apology languages with each other.

In this chapter, you journeyed through some intense relationship research, tools, and strategies. Your relationship with your partner is the independent variable in this entire stepfamily equation; all other factors rely on you two being together. It's critical that you have a strong bond built on respect, trust, and love. You're now ready for probably the most anticipated section of the entire book: control. In the next chapter, we'll discuss how to reclaim confident control as a stepmom, even when it feels impossible!

CHAPTER 8

Command Confident Control

It's time! You've finally made it to the chapter in the book that details how to command confident control as a stepmom. I hope you listened to me and didn't skip ahead, because by now, a foundation has been laid that enables you to embrace your control without concern of repercussions.

If your experience looks like mine as a stepmom, you have felt discouraged at all the ways stepfamily life feels out of your control. My schedule is predicated by a custody schedule. I live within a certain radius determined by the parenting plan. My partner and I don't have full control over our parenting; my stepdaughter's attitude, outlook, spirituality, and countless other things are greatly influenced by her mom 50% of the time.

There used to be a lot of trepidation around taking action: Would it cause her mom to be upset? Do we need her mom's permission? What if her mom wants to do it with her? These questions and the walking on eggshells constantly afraid of being taken to court again made me feel like I wasn't in control of my own life. I felt like Kevin, his ex-wife, and his daughter, had more of a say in decisions than I did. And for someone with a primary core value of control, that was tough.

In fact, it was this perceived lack of control that caused me to question the most if I could stay in this relationship. I'd think to myself, "Can I really take a backseat in my own life, for the rest of my life?" And if not obvious, the answer to that question was a resounding no. But instead of packing up my stuff, I got serious about figuring out how to find control in my stepmom life. This chapter is a detailed summary of everything I have learned and how I applied it to my life to feel confident that I am in control. Backseat no more!

This chapter begins with a deep dive into where you have complete control as a stepmom. You'll learn the difference between control and influence, because even when you can't have total control, you can still influence! Then, you'll discover the many ways you may be giving away your control.

Next, it's all about boundaries! This is one of my very favorite things to teach, and you'll soon see why. Boundaries, when structured correctly, will save you from resentment and protect your inner peace. You've learned what's in your control and what isn't, and boundaries are how you control something, even if it's not in your control. They're basically magical and life-changing and marriage-saving. You're welcome.

After you learn about boundaries and how to structure and communicate them, I'm going to give you some other very tangible ways of taking back control as a stepmom. I'll share some specific ex-related boundaries, like designating a space in your home as an ex-free zone, which gives you the freedom to have control over this space. You won't be surprised by a text or triggered by a conversation here. You can relax and be at home.

I'll teach you to work through how to take control of emotion-laden custody exchanges. Stepchildren are especially rambunctious (and often a bit combative) on transition days, and I'll share with you some great tips for taking control of this time. Finally, I'll teach you how to get real about how to stop living your life around the custody schedule. The custody schedule should not control you or your plans, and I'll get a bit soapbox-y trying to convince you too.

Control is within your reach, stepmom. You deserve confident control over your own life, and now it's yours for the taking. Let's dig in.

Embracing Your Control

*"If you don't like something, change it. If you can't change it,
change your attitude."*[53]

– Maya Angelou, author, poet, civil rights
activist, performer, and professor

One of the single biggest struggles across the board for stepmoms is
feeling like they lack control in their stepfamilies. In fact, I'm willing
to bet that you were tempted to skip ahead and read this chapter
first, after seeing it in the Table of Contents. Am I right?

Before you became a stepmom, you were an independent woman
with a life of your own. You were in charge of nearly every decision
in your life, big or small. You could decide where you wanted to
live, if you wanted to go on vacation, or what you wanted to eat for
dinner tonight. You likely didn't have to check with someone else
before scheduling a girls' night out or committing to a family outing.
You could unilaterally make decisions.

A lot of that changes when you become a stepmom. You now have
a partner, their children, a custody schedule, and a parenting plan to
consider. Your partner might give away control for the sake of "keeping the peace" with their child's other parent (more on this later in this
chapter). You might feel guilty for committing to that girls' night when
it's a night your partner has custody of their children. You might be
restricted to a radius of where you can live, as directed by your partner's custody agreement. It can feel like *so much* is out of your control.

I distinctly remember a conversation I had with my husband,
Kevin, several years ago when we were engaged to be married. We
were sitting outside the softball park where Krista was supposed to
be playing her game, but it was her weekend with her mom, and
her mom decided not to bring her to the game. Kevin and I had
awakened early and driven to the field, not knowing their plans
had changed. Understandably, I was fuming. I looked at him and
vented, "She makes me so angry!" Kevin, in his wise, obnoxiously
uber-positive way replied, "No one can make you angry. You have to
decide to let them affect you."

I'll be honest. That day at the ballpark, I wasn't ready for that advice. I rolled my eyes and muttered something about disrespect and selfishness, likely. But looking back, I see just how much I let her actions control my day, my mood, and my relationship. Admittedly, he was right.

It's easy to become overwhelmed by all the things you don't have control over. But in reality, as a stepmom, you have so much more control than you think you do.

CONTROL VERSUS INFLUENCE

I want you to think of control in the context of your dexterity. You have a dominant hand and a nondominant hand. (Unless you're ambidextrous, in which case, pretend you're not for the sake of the analogy.)

Your dominant hand can write legibly, throw a ball with relative accuracy, and shield you from incoming punches. In other words, you have complete control when you use your dominant hand.

Your nondominant hand is probably the one you use to write notes from the Elf on the Shelf or the tooth fairy. It's legible but less controlled than your natural handwriting. When you throw a ball with your nondominant hand, it doesn't go as far, and it doesn't always travel in the intended direction. The ball has made progress but didn't hit the target for which you intended. You can still shield an incoming punch with your nondominant hand, but you might not be as quick or effective with your defense. You'll have impact in defending yourself, but you won't have as much control as if you'd been able to use your dominant hand.

Given the choice, we would always use our dominant hand. Clearly, we have more control in these scenarios. We reach our goals, and our actions have their intended impact (e.g., throwing a ball and having it land in the other person's mitt instead of 3 ft away at the wrong angle).

But that's not always practical in every situation. We don't always have access to our dominant hand. Maybe it's already doing or holding something else. Maybe it hurts. Maybe the punch comes from the opposite side.

So, you roll with the (sometimes literal) punches and have what impact you can with your nondominant hand. Because some impact is better than none. You'd rather poorly shield a punch than let it land with full force. You'd rather get close in horseshoes than miss completely.

Some Impact Is Better Than None

In our stepfamilies, we have two hands. Sometimes, and with some things, we have full control. Other times, and with other things, we have influence. And yet sometimes, it's just out of our hands.

Let's take a practical look at these different categories:

Control:

I have complete control over:

◆ My actions
◆ My reactions
◆ My boundaries
◆ What I will say
◆ How I will spend my time
◆ What I will think about

Influence:

I have limited control but influence over:

◆ The boundaries my partner will set with the other parent (I can give my opinion, but my partner will set the boundary that feels right for them.)
◆ The house rules in my home (I can work with my partner to set the house rules, but I share the responsibility of enforcing them, which gives me limited impact.)
◆ The nutrition my stepchild will receive (I can cook a balanced meal, but I can't force-feed them.)
◆ The values my stepchild will grow up to believe are important (My impact is limited due to their other influences, but I can consistently role model the values I think are important for my stepchild.)

Everything Else:

I have little to no control or influence over:

◆ How another person will respond to my boundaries
◆ The screen time limits, rules, punishments, nutrition, and so on my stepchild receives in their other home
◆ What the ex will say about me
◆ What has already happened

Life isn't meant to be controlled 100% of the time. If it was, no one but you would have any autonomy. That's simply not a healthy dynamic in a stepfamily.

As a recovering control freak myself, I get it. I know how frustrating it can feel to have limited impact on the lives and behaviors of children who live in your home. I understand how infuriating it can be when your partner's ex uses their control and influence against you. But I also recognize how powerful your own control and influence can be when you fully harness this framework and maximize your own impact.

CONTROLLING YOUR MINDSET

My stepmom mantra is a quote by Poet Maya Angelou. She said, "If you don't like something, change it. If you can't change it, change your attitude."[53]

As a stepmom, I've experienced a lot of things I don't like. So, I do everything I possibly can to change the situation. I change every little thing I can, including setting crucial boundaries, until I can't change anything else. And once I've done all of that, I make the decision to control my mindset and change my attitude. Because I deserve peace and happiness more than the chaos deserves my attention.

Let's work through an example together. Let's pretend I am dealing with a co-parent with chronic tardiness. If I continue to get frustrated every time they're late for a drop-off, here's what I would change:

- ◆ I would stop making plans immediately after the planned custody exchange time. This will enable me to not be as stressed out about my co-parent arriving promptly. (I can control the plans I schedule.)
- ◆ I would stop being at the house or exchange point with my partner and decide to keep busy during this time instead. Me watching the clock doesn't help anyone to have less stress and more peace in this situation. (I can control where I will be.)
- ◆ I would encourage my partner to reiterate the importance of a prompt arrival to their ex. (My partner's communications with their ex is something I can influence.)

- ◆ I would set boundaries as necessary. (I can control my boundaries.)
- ◆ I would choose to prioritize my peace and not let the ex's actions affect my happiness. (I can control my mood.)

To summarize, when you find yourself stuck in a frustrating situation where you feel like you lack control, ask yourself, "What things can I control in this situation? What things can I influence?" and then repeat your stepmom mantra: "If you don't like something, change it. If you can't change it, change your attitude."[53]

To take things a step farther, I want you to ensure you aren't unintentionally and unnecessarily giving away control as a stepmom.

FOUR WAYS YOU'RE UNINTENTIONALLY GIVING AWAY CONTROL

Sometimes, stepmoms make the mistake of giving away the control that they desperately crave because they don't realize they're allowed to keep it! Here are the four most common examples I see in my work with stepmoms:

Not Empowering Your Partner to Make Decisions

This can happen a few different ways.

If you let the other parent make decisions unilaterally that should be made jointly, according to your parenting plan, then you're giving away control unnecessarily. Not to mention, opening yourself up to the opportunity to be disappointed or frustrated by their decision. All parenting plans are different of course, but your custody agreement should actually detail exactly which decisions need to be made jointly. Often, medical and educational decisions need to be agreed on by both parents.

Let's take an easy example under this umbrella: parent–teacher conferences. If you've been enabling your stepchild's other parent to schedule the parent–teacher conference for both parents to attend, only when it's convenient for the other parent, then you've given away control. Maybe you're trying to be considerate and flexible, choosing the path of least resistance. That's honorable but unnecessary.

A better approach would be to have your partner approach their co-parent, "Hey, these times work for me. Do any of these work for you too?" or request their availability so your partner can align with their schedule and move forward accordingly. Or to simply schedule a separate parent–teacher conference entirely that would enable your partner to have complete control over the scheduling.

Another way I see decision-making authority impact control when it shouldn't is by asking for permission on things your partner already has autonomy over.

In the beginning of my relationship with Kevin, I remember we would be overly considerate as a way to keep the peace and to try to be considerate co-parents. We wanted to do everything we could to avoid rocking the boat. An example of this kind of behavior was texting his ex to see if she approved of Krista watching a certain movie or TV show.

Your partner is an equal parent and has equal decision-making power. So, if you are giving away that decision, you are giving away their equal control and ability to make those decisions. You are actually unintentionally not empowering your partner. It's important to recognize that when we do things like this, despite our good intentions to keep the peace, it usually comes at the expense of our control and, ultimately, our peace.

Answering Messages or Calls from the Other Parent as They Come In, Instead of When It's the Best Time for You

If you are working your life around someone else needing your attention, you don't have full control over your life. I want you to start setting boundaries around this, so that you're fiercely protective of your time. If you're in the middle of preparing dinner, you don't need to stop what you're doing to reply to a text reminding you to wash and return your stepson's baseball uniform in two days. You're entitled to your time and your own priorities.

You don't need to pause your current task to accommodate someone else requesting your attention. I know that it can feel like you must stop what you're doing and give them a prompt response. I get it. I can remember feeling this way myself, but you don't have to. And the sooner you stop giving control away over your schedule to your stepchild's other parent, and everyone else, the better you'll feel!

And if they get upset by you not responding immediately? That's okay! If they want to become upset, they'll find a reason to get upset anyway.

Not Setting Boundaries to Protect Your Peace

Not setting boundaries robs you of control in a variety of ways. Setting boundaries enables you to protect yourself from others' ability to have control over your schedule, to have power over your emotions and who can affect you, and to remove yourself from triggering situations.

A common example of this I see is when a stepmom is overly involved with communication with the other parent. If you're the one communicating with your co-parent, you are giving them access to your day, your emotions, and your mental state. You're inadvertently giving away control.

Maybe you're thinking, "But if I don't do it, then my partner is going to have to, and they're toxic together! I'm so much better at communicating than they are. This is something I can do to help and support my partner." And that's admirable. It really is.

But at what cost?

You did have control over the fact that you were triggered by how the ex speaks to you, but you chose not to set a boundary, which gave away that control.

At what cost is trying to support your partner actually coming? Is it going to cost you your peace? Is it going to cost you control that you recognize you need in your life? If so, it's time to reclaim that control.

Planning Your Life Around a Custody Schedule

This example hits extremely hard for me because I was guilty of doing it for a very long time. When I first became a stepmom, when my stepdaughter was in our home, we were a family of three. I wasn't accepting invitations to go out for happy hour with my colleagues. I wasn't going to tutor my students or visiting my sister's house to hang out with her or my nephews. I was entirely focused on my family of three.

If an invitation arrived for something with the extended family, and we didn't have Krista on that day, or saw something fun that was coming up, but we didn't have her, we would decide not to go and decline the invitation.

Every decision about my time centered around my partner's custody schedule. It impacted every single decision that I made about how I spent my time, and in the process, I gave away so much control.

By deciding to live life around a custody schedule, I became extremely resentful that I was only seeing my nephews on certain days, or I was only going out with my friends on certain days, or I couldn't accept that invitation. It took so much control away from me. I would've shown up as a much better stepmom if I had just made plans without consideration for the custody schedule.

My stepdaughter's life is happening seven days a week. She's not living her life around a custody schedule, and I shouldn't be either. As a stepmom, you cannot live 100% of your life only 50% of the time.

You deserve to have complete control over your schedule. Your family won't suffer if you stop scheduling everything around the custody agreement. However, they will suffer if you become resentful from not prioritizing your own needs and desires. Your family needs the best version of you. You need control. So, take it back, for your sake, and for the sake of your family.

Activity: Survey Your Control

Take some time to reflect on the things in your life over which you have control and influence. Dig deep to include things here that you might be unnecessarily relinquishing control over. You might find the column formatting below helpful.

Things I Control	Things I Influence	Things to Let Go Of

The Basics of Boundaries

"If it costs you your peace, it's too expensive."
– Often attributed to Paulo Coelho, author of *The Alchemist*

I had no concept of personal boundaries when I first became a stepmom. Theoretically, I could tell you what the word meant. But when it came to practical implementation, I didn't know the first thing about boundaries.

I remember when my stepdaughter's mom moved in with us. (Yes, you read that correctly. She, her husband, and their daughter together lived with us for three months!) We heard many times, "Set boundaries! That's the only way this will work!" We quizzically looked at each other, saying, "But what does that mean?" and that, my friends, is how we wound up in that whole mess to begin with. If either of us had a healthy understanding of boundaries, we never would have lived all together in the first place!

Let's start with the simplest definition. Boundaries are what you are and are not okay with. Other people aren't mind readers, and each of us has different personal limits. This is why communicating what we are and are not comfortable with is critical for maintaining healthy relationships.

Boundaries are how we communicate what we need from others, but they're also a statement of how you will be treated. For example, you might need a boundary if your stepchild repeatedly disrespects you. You deserve respect, and you can set a boundary to communicate what you need from your stepchild and how you will be treated.

The great part about boundaries is that they don't require anyone's permission or compliance. You are in complete control of your boundaries, and you get to create the insulated healthy bubble in which you want to live.

IT'S OKAY TO TAKE UP SPACE

As a recovering people-pleasing codependent, I didn't know that I could say no; I didn't know that my needs mattered as much as everyone else's—that I'm an equal member of my family. They absolutely do, however. You don't meet someone with kids and automatically move to the back-burner position forever. And yet, that's the messaging society pushes down our throats a bit, yeah?

I'm here to tell you that it's okay–no, *necessary*–to take up space! My dear friend and fellow stepmom, Kait Hazlehurst, puts it this way:

When you first became a family with children, step or biological, you may have needed to trade your two-door coupe for a family sedan or an SUV, something that fit the car seats or had a third row. The kids took up space, and you had to accommodate it. Do you hate the kids for taking up space? Of course not. It just made sense to adjust to meet the needs of your family. So why are you afraid of taking up space? Why do you dread needing a seat and some legroom in the hypothetical car?[54]

It is imperative that you learn how to take up space by voicing your desires, needs, and boundaries in your stepfamily. "Sucking it up" and meeting everyone else's needs alone is not a sustainable way of living. You will suffer from burnout and resentment. And to be clear, neither of those is a suitable option. You deserve a life you love. You deserve to feel like you're an equal, respected member of your family. Not "just" the stepmom.

So, the next time you get an inkling that you don't want to do something, lean into the feeling. Is your stepdaughter telling stories about her other parent, and you feel uncomfortable or angry hearing them? Walk away. Say your stepson is suggesting that the whole family goes to check out the local Minecraft experience for the day, and you couldn't imagine anything worse to do. Veto the plan or stay home. Does the other parent want to celebrate birthdays and holidays together, but behind the scenes they're making your life a living hell? It's not worth your peace, so say, "No thanks!"

You get a voice, and you should use it.

WHAT A BOUNDARY IS AND IS NOT

Boundaries are how we take back control in a situation where it would've otherwise cost us our peace. Your number one priority as a stepmom is to manage your own peace of mind. Setting boundaries helps you to consistently maintain inner harmony.

Boundaries require self-awareness to recognize when you begin to feel uncomfortable and/or if your limit has been reached. Setting a boundary is setting the expectation for what you will do to protect your peace if it happens (again).

Here's a very simple example. If someone has called you and is yelling at you, you could decide that it's disrespectful, which is intolerable to you. An easy way to take back control, so that the other person cannot continue to affect your peace, is to hang up the phone. Same thing applies to the "block" function on your phone and social media. It exists for a reason. Use it!

A BOUNDARY IS ABOUT YOU

A boundary is not about the other person. The other person may do something that causes you to feel uncomfortable or makes it clear that a limit has been reached, but your boundary is about *you* and protecting *your* peace.

Boundaries will always be in first person, because you are the person that the boundary is protecting. It's not about keeping other people out; it's about protecting who's inside. A castle drawbridge comes down for invited guests, but it still keeps intruders out. Your boundaries are just like that: They don't repel everyone, but they do keep disrespectful people from entering your peace.

It's important that you start to take up space and get clarity on who you are, what you need, and what you deserve. You deserve a life of peace and respect. You're completely entitled to boundaries that protect that peace. Once you start to embrace this shift, your boundaries will become more apparent. With practice, you'll get more aligned with your needs and become better at setting effective boundaries that protect you.

A BOUNDARY IS NOT A REQUEST

Many people think having a boundary is asking another person to stop or start doing something. That's actually just a request. The request is important, because if the person honors the request, a boundary may not be necessary, but the request itself is not a boundary.

A true boundary is in complete control of the person making the boundary, which is why it's so empowering. If you've not had luck with people respecting your boundaries in the past, it's likely because you've been phrasing them as requests. You are entitled to more control than that! You don't need others to comply with your requests because you are in control of your own boundaries.

A request resembles, "Hey babe, can you please have the kids take their nightly call with their other parent in another room?" But a boundary sounds like, "Hey babe, can you please have the kids take their nightly call with their other parent in another room? If not, I'll spend some time in our room until they're off the phone."

If hearing the other parent's voice or their conversations upsets you, you don't have to sit idly by. You are not destined to live a life of resentment simply because you're a stepmom. You are entitled to your boundaries, so take steps to mitigate resentment and protect your peace.

A BOUNDARY IS NOT A RULE

With rules, the onus is on the other person to comply. An example of a rule is: All family members have good table manners. You're expecting others to comply with the stated rule. Boundaries, on the other hand, place the onus on you to enforce the boundary. An example of a boundary is: "Hey babe, can you please encourage your kids to have better manners at the dinner table? Until they're able to chew with their mouths closed and not talk with food in their mouths, I'll need to eat in my office."

If sitting at the dinner table is disrupting your peace and affecting your relationship, stop doing it! You aren't at the mercy of others to comply with house rules. You are in control!

A BOUNDARY IS NOT AN ULTIMATUM

The big difference here is in the motive behind the statement.

An ultimatum is often stated with the intention of guilting or manipulating someone into doing what you want them to do. I've heard stepmoms threaten to end the relationship if they don't get their way. If that's a true non-negotiable for you, then definitely communicate it to your partner. But if you have no intention of leaving the relationship over the issue, don't give your partner an ultimatum. That's simply not a loving or respectful way to communicate.

A boundary prioritizes your peace and your relationship over the situation. It says, "I wish this would be the decision you'd make, but if it's not, my peace of mind and us having a happy, healthy relationship are my top priorities."

An ultimatum divides, while a boundary connects. An ultimatum is manipulative, while a boundary is protective.

A BOUNDARY CREATES HEALTHIER RELATIONSHIPS

Finally, in case it wasn't clear, setting boundaries is a way to have better, stronger relationships. There are two main reasons why:

1. Boundaries protect you from resentment.
2. Boundaries enable people to get to know and love the real you.

Boundaries Protect You from Resentment

When other people disrespect you, it inevitably leads to negative feelings like frustration, disappointment, and anger. When it happens enough, it can easily morph into resentment. This is especially risky for stepmoms because resentment often becomes directed at our partners, not only the person disrespecting us.

Your relationship deserves to be protected from other people's disrespectful behavior. Your partner deserves the respect of knowing that someone else's actions won't drive a wedge between you. Your relationship deserves a fighting chance, and as long as you lack boundaries with other people, you don't have that fighting chance. Protect yourself from resentment with healthy boundaries, and you're ultimately protecting your relationship in the process. It's a win-win!

Boundaries Allow People to Get to Know and Love the Real You

The more self-aware you are, the better boundaries you'll set. The better boundaries you set, the more authentically and genuinely you show up in your relationships. By presenting clear boundaries, you are interacting as your true self–no eggshells, no masks–simply pure, unadulterated YOU. It's a gift to those around you–the ability to get to know and to love the real you.

When we have boundaries, we can have deeper, more respectful, and loving relationships. Our relationships are then built on a solid foundation of love and respect.

Activity: Assess Your Boundary Needs

Start taking inventory of where you might need to set boundaries. Where have you been tolerating behavior that you're not okay with? Next, you'll learn how to structure a great boundary. For now, get your boundary needs list started!

Structuring Impenetrable Boundaries

"Daring to set boundaries is about having the courage to love ourselves, even when we risk disappointing others."[55]
– Brené Brown, author, researcher, professor, and motivational speaker

You've learned what a boundary is, and what it isn't. Now, we get to my favorite part: setting them! I've come a long way since those "Yes, your ex can live with us" days, and I'm thrilled to share what I've learned about setting impenetrable boundaries with you.

I've helped clients create boundaries for countless situations, but one that requires perhaps the most delicacy involves money. Stepmoms everywhere are fielding requests for extra child support. At the same time, their partners are managing their guilt for wanting to support their children and give them the life they deserve, while also protecting their partners and keeping them happy.

Here's how I would communicate a boundary to Kevin if I disagree with how money is spent:

> Babe, I know you love me and always work to make me feel protected and respected in our relationship. And I am happy to share finances with you. However, when I don't get a say in financial decisions, or when I feel like others are taking advantage of you/us in terms of money, it makes me feel negatively toward that person, and it creates conflict in our relationship. Can you please discuss financial matters with me, and let's make decisions together? If financial decisions continue to be made without my input, then, in order to protect our relationship and my peace, I am going to pull out $x for a separate account.

Notice how I'm setting a boundary that is about protecting my relationship, not punishing my husband. It's also entirely about what I will do and not establishing a rule that requires compliance by him. I've properly communicated to him why I believe the boundary is necessary, and what I will be doing. It isn't a vague statement of requests or intentions, and it has been communicated directly to the person affected. I didn't tell the other parent to stop asking for money, I didn't tell my husband to stop sending money (though I can absolutely express my concerns and make a request of him). Instead, I chose to set a boundary to protect my peace of mind (and my income), when I couldn't control other people.

When you're ready to set a boundary, remember "WAIT." WAIT is an easy acronym to help you remember the four crucial components of communicating an impenetrable boundary. It stands for

Why

Ask

If

Then

WHY

Give the person to whom you are communicating your boundary the reason why that boundary is necessary. What is the result of not having that boundary currently? What will being protected offer you? Why should this person care about your need for this boundary?

In the earlier example, I said, "When I don't get a say in financial decisions, or when I feel like others are taking advantage of you/us in terms of money, it makes me feel negatively toward that person, and it creates conflict in our relationship."

Our partners don't want us to feel negatively about their children especially, and they definitely don't want conflict in our relationships. Letting them know what this boundary will solve helps them to understand our perspective and hopefully get on board with the idea.

ASK

Make a request! Ask the person you're setting a boundary with to do what you'd like them to do. The request is an important part of the boundary because if it's honored, the boundary isn't necessary.

I asked my husband in our fictional example, "Can you please discuss financial matters with me, and let's make decisions together?"

He is invited to change. He's been given the information to know why I am making the request, and now he can decide the best right course of action for him. It is just as important for my partner to protect his peace as it is for me to protect mine. He doesn't have to honor my request if it misaligns with his values and priorities (which is why this chapter on boundaries is critical!).

IF, THEN

If the person you are communicating your boundary to doesn't want to or isn't capable of honoring your request, then you must start setting an enforceable boundary. What will you do to protect your peace if your request isn't respected? How will you reclaim peace when someone else is making a decision that is affecting you?

This might not be the optimal outcome. Your boundary may be the next-best alternative to your preferred choice, but it's definitely better than resentment or conflict.

My example boundary was, "If financial decisions continue to be made without my input, then, in order to protect our relationship and my peace, I am going to pull out $x for a separate account."

This boundary is entirely in my control. It's what I will do. In this fictitious example, I will pull money out of my paycheck and put it into a separate account, so I have total control over how it's spent. I will have peace of mind knowing that not all my hard-earned money is going to support my stepchild's other parent who I perceive to be irresponsible with our finances. I would prefer that my partner honor my request, but if he can't, this is a way to take back control and protect my peace.

I'm not doing this to punish my husband or to manipulate or guilt him into doing what I want him to do. I have shared with him my reasons and my request. I value our relationship over the conflict, so I communicate and enforce a clear boundary to protect us.

ADDITIONAL EXAMPLES

I hesitate to include this section because I don't want you to think that these are the only if/then options, but if I'm going to hold true to my promise of stepmomming made easy, then I think it's important to give you a few more common examples of boundaries stepmoms need to set.

These are examples of *how* you can tackle these stressors, not the *only* way to structure your boundary. How you protect your peace may look differently than how I would do it. That's perfectly natural! Refine your "why." Make the request that you need. Change up your if/then options to match what would give you the most peace. This is a jumping off point, not the destination.

Okay, now that we've gotten that out of the way, here are some more common stepmom boundaries examples for you!

When the Other Parent Sends Harassing or Excessive Texts

To be clear, you aren't responsible for communicating with your stepchild's other parent. That is primarily your partner's co-parent, not yours. You don't owe the other parent any communication if it costs you your peace.

Why: "Hi, your texts are harassing/excessive/rude. I am unable to allow you to continue disrespecting me."

Ask: "Please only communicate respectfully/when necessary, with pertinent information."

If/Then: "If you choose not to honor my wishes, I will block your number and be unavailable for future communications."

Unless your parenting plan specifically requires it, you are not required to keep lines of communication open with the other parent. You're perfectly entitled to a boundary of blocking their number if they do not honor your request for respectful communication.

When Your Partner Won't Enforce the Kids Being Responsible for Chores

Why: "Babe, I know you work incredibly hard to provide for our family, and I appreciate that so much. But sometimes it gets to be a lot taking care of everything around the house, especially when the kids are home with us and there's more to clean up."

Ask: "I know you don't think the kids should have to do chores in our home but not getting any help from them with cleanup is really starting to make me feel resentful. Would you be willing to have the kids do the dishes three times per week?"

If/Then: "If you're not comfortable with that, then, in order for me to feel better about the situation and not feel resentful toward anyone in our family, I'll be hiring a maid to help with dishes and laundry during our custodial time."

You're letting your partner know that you appreciate their contribution to the home, while also being honest about why it's necessary for a change. It is most important that you protect your peace and set boundaries, instead of conceding to what is working for others. Their comfort shouldn't come at the expense of yours.

Boundaries are an incredible tool for reclaiming control and prioritizing your mental wellness. They enable you to prevent others' actions from affecting you. As a stepmom, it's so easy to feel like others have control in your life; boundaries are your saving grace.

Activity: Structure Your Boundaries Using the WAIT Framework

Review the list you created earlier in this chapter of opportunities to set boundaries, pick your most crucial boundaries, and structure them using the WAIT framework.

Ex-Free Zone and Other Ex-Related Boundaries

"People may get angry at us for setting boundaries; they can't use us anymore."[56]

– Melody Beattie, author of *Codependent No More*

Now that you've begun mastering the art of boundaries, there's one person you're probably dying to get started with: your stepchild's other parent. Unless you have full custody and don't co-parent, of course, in which case, this section isn't for you! You have my rare permission to skip ahead, my friend!

Co-parenting can cause a lot of lines to become blurred. One parent is purchasing clothes for both homes. One parent is taking the kids for haircuts without asking or informing the other parent beforehand. One parent is signing the kids up for extracurricular activities that the other parent will be responsible for paying half of and taking the children to half of the time. Each household can make decisions that affects the other, without always getting buy-in on those decisions. To avoid resentment from this chaos, set boundaries to protect your peace.

I recommend setting these three boundaries, at a minimum:

◆ When and for how long you'll communicate about the other parent
◆ Not being connected with the other parent on social media
◆ Not trash-talking your partner with their ex

EX-RELATED BOUNDARY #1: WHEN AND FOR HOW LONG YOU'LL COMMUNICATE ABOUT THE OTHER PARENT

It can feel exhausting thinking and/or talking about the other parent all the time. Setting boundaries around certain hours you will allow that conversation to occur, or for how long each day you will talk about it, helps to take back control in a situation that could easily feel out of control. Their actions won't dictate your mood or your entire day; *you* will take back control of your time and energy.

There are a few ways that you can implement time boundaries. Explore which of these may work best for you and your partner.

Business Hours: Set defined "business hours" for when you will discuss the ex, court, and so forth. If a text from the other parent, an email from your lawyer, or stray thought pops into your head during any other hour of the day, you should dismiss it and wait until your next block of "business hours" with your partner.

For example, I have a client who designated 9–11 a.m. and 2–4 p.m. as their "business hours." They protected their mornings, ensuring a peaceful wakeup and getting the kids off to school. In addition, they protected their evenings, not allowing the other parent to derail their family time.

Daily Time Limit: Set a timer for how long you'll discuss the ex, court, and so forth, per day. Start and stop the timer with your discussions. If you're in the thick of heavy conflict, your timer might need to be higher, like two hours. But if you're able to keep it even lower, like 15 or 30 minutes, just think of how much more time you'll have for doing things that bring you peace! Just imagine the mood shift.

"Keep It Concise" Agreement: If it's necessary to discuss new things as they arise, but you don't want to allow the conflict to rule your day, you might need a "Keep It Concise" Agreement instead. Set a 5-20 minute timer every time a new discussion of the other parent or conflict begins. When the timer is up, the conversation is over. Your peace is more important than continuing that conversation.

Bonus Spatial Boundary: Designate an ex-free zone in your home where you will make the conscious decision not to think about, talk about, or communicate with the other parent. You deserve a space where you feel protected and are able to let your guard down.

I once had a client who was lying in bed with her new fiancé and asked him a lot of questions about his prior relationship. She wanted to know about the good times and the bad, their connection–even their sex life. She asked several questions in their bed, and she could never un-hear the answers. Protect your relationship *and* your space.

You might choose to have a time and spatial boundary or only one. There's no wrong answer. Try out various options to see which works best for you.

EX–RELATED BOUNDARY #2: NOT BEING CONNECTED WITH THE OTHER PARENT ON SOCIAL MEDIA

Being connected on social media often creates more drama than it does connection. I totally respect that it can be nice to see pictures of your stepchildren when they're not with you. But what is it costing you?

I once had a stepmom friend who got into unnecessary conflict because of Facebook. They'd had a great day as a family, and after tucking her stepdaughters into bed and getting settled, her partner published a sweet post with photos reflecting on their fun. His ex, seeing the post late at night tagged at the location, was irate. How dare he keep the kids up so late! She fired off an angry text, which only annoyed my friend and her partner.

I've had several clients complain to me about how the ex posts on social media as if they're the Parent of the Year, but they know the truth. Maybe the photos were actually taken by the stepmom. Maybe the other parent just ghosted their parental time and disappointed their child again. Maybe they really do love to post every single time they're with their child, and the stepmom is reading into it. Regardless, it's all unnecessary conflict.

A few years back, I wasn't following my own advice, and Facebook initiated a fun new feature that notifies you when one of your friends interacts with another friend's content. I don't have to tell you how annoying it was to be alerted that a member of my husband's family had commented on a photo of my husband's ex-wife.

I stand by my statement: It causes more drama than it does connection, for a variety of reasons. Just say no!

EX-RELATED BOUNDARY #3: NOT TRASH-TALKING YOUR PARTNER WITH THEIR EX

Perhaps it seems obvious that you wouldn't trash-talk your partner with their ex, but I've seen it occur a few times. It seems harmless to bond with them over a small grievance. It might even feel validating to bond over your partner leaving their socks all over the home. The ex is perhaps the only other person who really gets it. But they're not the right audience. Your partner needs (and deserves) your loyalty.

Of course, this list isn't exhaustive. If you have another boundary you want to set with or relating to the other parent, you have my full permission to do so. This list is meant to get you started on your boundary-setting journey.

Activity: Create Co-Parent Boundaries

Consider what boundaries you need to set with your stepchild's other parent. Have you allowed lines to get blurred? Where can you draw a clear line with your boundaries?

Establish Transition Rituals

> *"If you talk about it, it's a dream, if you envision it, it's possible, but if you schedule it, it's real."*[57]
>
> – Tony Robbins, Life Coach,
> motivational speaker, and author

Custody transitions can be emotionally charged and disruptive for everyone in the family. I've met many stepmoms who dread custody transitions because of how tumultuous they can be. It's like the stepchildren forget how the house functions when they've been away.

They don't follow the rules, they're emotional, and they're resistant and standoffish. Of course you dread them coming home, and everything that comes with it.

We're essentially asking our stepchildren to "flip a switch" between homes and parents. Imagine uprooting your life every-other-week or so, switching to a different home, different bedroom, different house rules, different dinner time and bedtime, different pets and siblings … on top of the emotional experience we already discussed like missing Parent A, feeling guilty for feeling that way when with Parent B, struggling to share their parent with a stepparent and maybe also step- or half-siblings. One of the best ways I've learned to ease custody trade-offs is by implementing transition rituals.

Scheduling Smoother Transitions

Whenever possible, transitions that occur at an activity are best. For example, Parent A drops the child off at school on Friday, and Parent B picks them up from school. This way, the child has time to adjust to not seeing Parent A and is able to be fully focused on Parent B at pickup. There's no emotional pull between parents, no guilt for being excited, and no sadness saying goodbye to Parent A.

While those of us who transition at school or other activities still experience emotion-laden transitions, they're not nearly as disruptive as those occurring in-person with both original parents.

Ease those transitions between homes by creating rituals to welcome the kids home in a peaceful way. Plan a fun game, a dinner that's guaranteed to be a hit, or start a TV series as a family. Do this same activity each transition to help them "flip the switch." They'll recognize the activity and be reminded which house they're at, and why they enjoy it so much.

Further, I encourage stepmoms to designate a transition ritual of their own ahead of custody exchanges. Do things that recharge you and leave you feeling more peaceful and fulfilled before your stepchildren come home. Prepare yourself with the gift of extra peace before the transition.

And if your personal transition ritual and the family transition ritual still aren't enough to make things feel peaceful, you can always excuse yourself from the chaos.

I worked with a stepmom client who knew that transitions with her two stepchildren were utter chaos and designated those nights as laundry night. She'd put her young children to bed, then sneak into her bedroom to fold clothes and watch reality TV. Her stepchildren appreciated the time with just their dad to transition back to their home, and their stepmom enjoyed time away from the emotionally charged interactions. It was a win-win!

Get in the habit of running transitions smoothly instead of letting them run you.

Activity: Brainstorm Family Transition Rituals

Brainstorm possible transition rituals to do as a family. What is something unique to your family or a guaranteed good time?

Activity: Implement a Personal Transition Ritual

Decide on a personal transition ritual. What will help you feel more peaceful and ready for transition day? Schedule it!

Stop Living 100% of Your Life 50% of the Time

"You are not a product of your circumstances. You are a product of your decisions."[58]

– Stephen R. Covey, author of *The 7 Habits of Highly Effective People*

I used to let the custody schedule dictate our lives. I would decline invitations to adult get-togethers that fell on the nights we had my stepdaughter, Krista. If family invitations fell on the days we didn't have her, we'd graciously decline. I planned outings, vacations, and crafts for the days we had her. And on the days that she was at her mom's, I stayed at work late, got caught up on my master's schoolwork, and maybe made time for a date night.

I made sure everything was fun and that our schedule was filled when my stepdaughter was with us. And I did my best not to do fun things without her, so she wouldn't feel left out. I thought that was how life as a stepmom with shared custody was supposed to be. But it left me burned out, exhausted, and honestly, a little resentful. I was living my life around a schedule someone else set.

I learned an important lesson at this point in my stepmom journey. If you want a successful relationship and a stepmom life you love, then you cannot live 100% of your life 50% of the time. Am I sad that my stepdaughter misses out on some things now that we've started living our life 100% of the time? Of course, I am. But the reality is, my stepdaughter's life doesn't end when she leaves our home. She's not living her life 50% of the time ... so why were we?

YOUR KIDS NEED A POSITIVE EXAMPLE OF A HEALTHY RELATIONSHIP

A key part of our responsibility as parents is to role model healthy skills for our children. One of those key skills is to relate to others in a healthy, kind, and fulfilling way. Your stepchildren are looking to you to show them what a healthy relationship looks like. That includes kind communication, prioritization of connection time (like date night), loving affection, and a teamwork attitude.

Showing the kids that your relationship is the first priority (even though sometimes the kids need to be your first responsibility), helps them to understand how to structure their family for success when they're older. Checking out of the relationship when the kids come back to your home does a complete disservice to them.

Further, giving them positive, loving examples of fiercely protected boundaries ensures they'll feel comfortable setting boundaries to protect themselves when necessary. Living your life and being present in your relationship 24/7, not only on the days when you don't have the kids, is actually one of the best things you can do for your kids.

YOU PUT AN UNREASONABLE BURDEN ON YOUR STEPKIDS TO BE "ON" AND RESPONSIBLE FOR YOUR HAPPINESS

When you are living your life fully during custodial time, you are (inadvertently) sending your stepchildren the wrong message. You are communicating to them that your life revolves around them, and they are responsible for your happiness. Not only does this lead to a whole host of other concerns, including parentification, codependency, mini-wife syndrome, entitled children who think the world revolves around their desires, and so forth, it also places an unreasonable burden on them as kids. It's the burden to be "on" energetically for you every time they're in your home.

If they're having a bad day, feeling sick, or just generally not feeling it one day, which is completely normal, they're being taught to put a smile on anyway because their parent has been waiting for them to come home. They begin to believe they're responsible for your happiness and being present in order for you to live your life. But really, their focus should be on their own happiness and living their own lives.

IT REINFORCES THE FEELING THAT YOU LIVE TWO SEPARATE LIVES

Planning your life around a custody schedule can clearly impact your stepchildren and your relationship, but this arrangement also negatively affects a stepmom's mental health. Feeling like all the "fun" things needed to be reserved for when Krista was home made me feel sometimes like she was more worthy of the event than I was. Shouldn't our relationship, me, be enough to warrant some fun on the noncustodial days too?

Turning away invitations to see family or friends because it didn't fall during the "right" time of our custody schedule eventually made me feel like I was missing out. When that became a pattern, it ultimately led to resentment. It frustrated me that my plans were being determined (indirectly) because my partner had a child with someone else.

Living half of the time with a devoted partner and autonomy over decisions and half of the time completely focused on the kids, means that who you are, who you're surrounded with, and what your priorities are one day might look dramatically different than the next. It's extremely challenging to navigate. And if that challenge affects your life enough, it could easily lead to resentment, typically directed at your partner.

Make a conscious decision not to live your life around the custody schedule. Accept the invitations. Go on the date, no matter if it's an "on" or "off" day. Balance your workload so that it doesn't pile up on days you get your partner to yourself. Refuse to live your life in response to the custody agreement–in response to your partner's past. You'll be really glad you did.

Activity: Journal About Your Scheduling Decisions

Reflect on how you've let the custody schedule influence your decisions. Have you been treating custodial time differently than noncustodial time?

How does it feel to be more in control?! Life-changing? Sanity-saving? I love teaching about control because I remember how crippling it felt to think I didn't have any in my stepfamily. You've made so much progress already, but there's one piece of the puzzle left: a supportive network that really understands what you're going through. No one gets it like another stepmom, so in the next chapter, we're exploring the final step of the Forever Formula: Seek Validating Support.

CHAPTER 9

Seek Validating Support

You've made it through the bulk of the book now, and I am so proud of you. You've learned life-changing and relationship-saving tools, but they will only get you so far. Without first working through your emotional response, you'll be unable to move through to the logical phase of analyzing the situation and determining how to move forward.

The tools that you've read about and developed while reading this book will help you resolve nearly any stepfamily stressor you might encounter. Yet, there's still a need for validating support. In laymen's terms: Sometimes you just need to vent to someone! And that's perfectly OK! I teach other stepmoms how to have a life of peace and sustainable happiness in their blended families, and I'd be lost without a stepmom bestie to vent to some days.

In this chapter, you'll discover the importance of a stepmom support person, and I'll give you some tips for how to find your new stepmom friend who really gets it!

The Importance of a Support Network

*"Contact with another person is a basic biological need;
loneliness is a form of starvation."*[35]
> – Emily Nagoski, PhD, and Amelia Nagoski,
> DMA, co-authors of *Burnout: The Secret to
> Unlocking the Stress Cycle*

No one gets it like another stepmom. If they did, stepmoms would never hear "You knew what you were signing up for." It would be the end of the stepmom double standard, and I'd be out of a job.

As much as I would love for your mom, your sister, your therapist, and your closest girlfriend since childhood to understand and validate your experience, unless they've been a stepmom themselves, they simply can't. Even your partner who's in the same family and experiences the same stepfamily dynamics as you do cannot fully understand your perspective as a stepmom. Another stepmom, however? She just gets it.

She understands the feelings that you're ashamed to admit. She knows how lonely you feel sometimes, even when you're surrounded by people. She recognizes how your home sometimes just doesn't feel like home. A fellow stepmom knows that sometimes you are damned if you do, and damned if you don't.

She can listen to you without judging or trying to solve (or minimize) your problems. She will empathize and normalize your experiences. Your relationship will be deeper than other new friendships because it's built on a foundation of shared stepmom experiences.

THE RISK OF AN UNTRAINED THERAPIST

I'm a staunch advocate for mental health and believe everyone can benefit from therapy. However, I advise stepmoms to ensure that their therapist has been trained in blended family dynamics before discussing their stepmom struggles. Too many times, I've seen untrained professionals offer advice that does more harm than good, leaving the stepmom feeling worse off than she did before she entered the therapist's care. I firmly believe these therapists were well-meaning, but the advice you can give a mom in a nuclear family simply isn't the same advice that you should give a stepmom.

I've compiled all the advice that my stepmom clients have heard from their therapists in sessions which only made them feel more guilty and more discouraged than ever. My hope is that by sharing these stories, you'll recognize any bad advice you've received from well-meaning but ill-equipped support people in your life, and then surround yourself with an understanding group who gets it.

The first piece of advice many of my stepmom clients have heard from their therapist or counselor before me is, "The kids need to come first in the family." And while that is an okay and standard bit of advice for traditional families (although I'm not totally convinced), when we're speaking about a stepfamily, that is simply not a sustainable foundation.

For stepmom relationships, the parent-child relationship usually existed before the relationship between the two partners. And in that way, it did come first. Yet, that doesn't make that relationship the top priority. I believe firmly that as a couple, you must be a strong foundation for your family. Your relationship as a couple must be the top priority, but sometimes the kids need to be the first responsibility. Let me say that again: The relationship needs to be the first priority, but sometimes the children need to be the first responsibility.

When your kids really need you, you need to be available to them but generally speaking, your partnership needs to be the foundation of the family, and the kids cannot come first. Let's look at an example. Pretend it's a Friday night, and my husband and I have a date night planned. We've booked the sitter, made the dinner reservation, and we're dressed and ready to go. We're going to show our children that nurturing our relationship is important and give them a positive example of a healthy marriage. Then, about an hour before the sitter arrives, my stepdaughter looks at my husband and says, "Hey, Dad, I really want to hang out with you tonight. Can you stay home instead and play video games with me?" While I love that my stepdaughter wants to spend time with her dad, this evening our relationship needs to be the top priority. Date night will go on as planned. However, if an hour before date night, my stepdaughter breaks her arm, then we are obviously cancelling date night and taking her to the emergency room. At that point, of course, she is our first responsibility.

The second piece of advice a stepmom coaching client has relayed to me from their therapist was essentially that the stepmom needed to "suck up" her feelings. The therapist probably phrased it in a much kinder way, but my response to that is an unapologetic "Hell no!" Your feelings are valid; your experiences are valid. My advice as your stepmom coach is never going to be to "suck it up" or to get over it.

> Emotions are simply biological signals designed to nudge you in the direction of beneficial change. ... When it comes down to it, if you feel crappy it's because your brain is telling you that there's a problem that's unaddressed or unresolved. In other words, negative emotions are a call to action.
> – *Mark Manson, author of The Subtle Art of Not Giving a F*ck*[59]

Your feelings exist for a reason; ignoring them is futile, they need resolution. I think this is absolutely one of those stigmas around stepparenting. Non-stepmoms just don't get it. They do not understand what you are going through or how complex and challenging your stepmom role and the associated emotions are.

Along the same lines, the third piece of advice that a client stated a previous therapist has given them is, "Do not share your feelings with your partner. They have enough going on. Let them tackle that, and you work on your own feelings." Frankly, all these years later, I'm still at a loss for words at this advice. Your partner is the only person who can make all this worth it. You should absolutely be able to rely on them with your feelings. Of course, you should talk to your partner! It's absurd to say that you shouldn't.

Now, I'm not suggesting that you vent to your partner about every little thing. Of course not. You can vent to your stepmom bestie or coach. Stepmoms don't need to bring every little thing to their partners. But to say that you shouldn't share how you're feeling or how your partner's actions or stepchildren's actions are affecting you? That's ridiculous and detrimental.

Please, stepmoms, seek a professional who is trained in working with stepfamilies, especially a therapist who is a fellow stepmom if possible. Because as you know, no one gets it like another stepmom.

Activity: Assess Your Existing Network

Take some time to brainstorm about any stepmoms you already know! Maybe it's an aunt, a cousin, or a colleague that can relate because they're a stepmom too. Who do you already know that gets it? Reach out to them for support.

How to Find Other Stepmoms to Connect With

"Friendship is born at that moment when one person says to another, 'What! You too? I thought I was the only one.'"[60]
    – C.S. Lewis, author of *The Lion, The Witch,
and the Wardrobe*

You know it's important to find other stepmoms to connect to, but the actual process of finding them can be challenging. There aren't many stepmoms shouting from the rooftops about their role. There's no lettermen jacket or class ring being handed out for stepmoms to proudly wear. They're taught to put on a brave face, so you might not even recognize another stepmom if you see her out in the wild.

Don't fret! Through the years, I have learned several ways to find other stepmoms with whom to connect. Your community of people who get it is closer than you think. The following are some examples of how to find your supporters.

JOIN A FACEBOOK GROUP FOR STEPMOMS

If you visit https://www.facebook.com/groups/ and search for the keyword "stepmom," you'll find dozens of resources centering around stepmoms. Note, not all stepmom Facebook groups are created equally, so I encourage you to actively monitor how you feel when interacting with their posts. If you start to forget the lessons that you learned in this book, or begin to feel extra irritated or resentful, leave the group. Some stepmoms are only ready to commiserate, and not yet ready to create the change they want to see and need.

I run a Facebook group called Stepmomming Ain't Easy. Our moderator team works hard to keep it a supportive group for stepmoms seeking personal growth. You can find it at: https://www.facebook.com/groups/stepmommingainteasy. Actually, I met one of my best friends in real life (IRL) in this group!

This type of group can be a tremendous asset when you're feeling alone in your experiences and feelings and need to be validated.

SEARCH FOR STEPMOMS IN YOUR LOCAL FACEBOOK GROUP

Search Facebook Groups for groups located in your local community and join those that seem relevant. For example, I'm a member of Frisco Residents Who Care and Moms of Frisco because I'm located in Frisco, Texas. I'm also a member of the Facebook group exclusively for my neighborhood. If you aren't already part of your local Facebook groups, search them out. They're valuable for gaining information about your area quickly and easily.

I recommend that you join a few and start by creating a new post. Something along the lines of, "Hey, I'm Kristen! Any other stepmoms here?" will suffice. Then, see who responds and ask to connect with them offline. Meet for coffee or a glass of wine. You might just click with your new best friend.

NEXTDOOR

Nextdoor is not only for National Weather Alerts and asking, "Were those gunshots?" on Independence Day. The app is actually great for connecting with people near you. It's a similar suggestion to the Facebook group idea, but it's a different audience potentially! Why not try downloading the app and seeing if any of your neighbors are also stepmoms? I bet they could use community as much as you could!

MEETUP

Meetup, if you're unfamiliar with it, is an app for people to meet over shared interests. Not every market area has a stepmom group, but several of them do! And if your area doesn't already have one, think about starting your own local support group.

COACHING GROUPS LIKE SERENITY + SISTERHOOD

If you're looking for community and professional support, I highly recommend joining a group coaching program. My program is called Serenity + Sisterhood, and my two goals are obvious: to give you peace and to help you find your stepmom sisterhood. In this program, you can get real-life support, feedback, and advice, in addition to communing with other stepmoms in your shoes. It's a win–win!

Activity: Find a New Stepmom Friend

Choose whichever recommendation from this chapter you prefer, and then take that step to find a stepmom friend you can talk to on those difficult days when you just need an empathetic ear.

Sweet stepmom, you've done it. You've mastered the final step of the Forever Formula: building a network of women to support you on your challenging stepmom days. You've surrounded yourself with people who will say, "Oh man, I totally get how you feel" and will encourage you to stick to your boundaries. You've built a network that will enable you to tune out the "You knew what you were signing up for" and "Just suck it up" counterproductive, ignorant comments. You're that much closer to a stepmom life you love!

CHAPTER 10

Go Live a Stepmom Life You Love

Hey girl, you made it! I am so proud of you. This book was a doozie, chock-full of activities forcing you to do a lot of introspection and make a lot of uncomfortable changes. But you made it to the end, through the six steps of the Forever Formula, toward a brighter future.

We haven't eliminated the double standard or reversed the "evil stepmom" trope. You won't ever be able to anticipate everything you could personally experience as a stepmom. However, now you're equipped with the tools needed to manage whatever stepfamily life may throw at you and reclaim your peace. Stepmomming certainly isn't easy, but by using this book, you now have the right tools to make it easy.

When you're faced with a situation that could affect you, ask yourself, "Which option will give me the most peace?" and follow that path. Set boundaries and claim control. Do what is necessary to protect your peace.

Remember your top three priorities in this order:

1. Your peace of mind
2. Your relationship
3. Your family

If you desire a stepmom life that you love, you cannot give to others until you have first taken care of yourself. Prioritizing your peace of mind is the best thing you can do for your family, so check that guilt at the door. Only do those things you can do graciously, without expectation.

Continue to prioritize self-care (especially exercise, which completes the stress cycle and mitigates burnout). Take time to prioritize the self-care that helps make you, *you*. Stepmomming is what you do, it's not who you are. When you balance the stepmom part of your life with your other responsibilities and passions, you're able to be the best stepmom you can be.

In addition, prioritize couple-care. Your partner is the only person who can compensate for all the additional stressors and complexities of stepfamily life that you'll experience. Pour energy into your relationship and enjoy your partner!

I've done a decent job avoiding my soapbox for over 200 pages, but a girl can only contain herself so long when she's this passionate! I'm certain you've heard the term "real mom" (as opposed to stepmom), and I want to address this before you to go out into the world a better, more peaceful stepmom. In fact, I've received my fair share of ignorant comments and had to fake a smile while having "real mom" comments said to my face more times than I count. I need you to know that I see you, stepmom. You are a real parent with real feelings. Every part of your role is indeed real.

The parenting you do is real. Your sacrifice is real. You are not a part-time parent, a temporary parent, or a non-parent. You are a very real influence in your stepchild's life, and you are 100% real.

You haven't given birth to your stepchild, but that doesn't make your contribution less real than that of an original parent. While you didn't have an automatic biological connection, you did earn that connection by spending real time together. You give to your family in different, but no less real or important, ways.

You are a real parent, and you are making a real difference. Go live a stepmom life you love, my friend. Tune out the noise!

References

1. Marine, Jennifer Newcomb, and Carol Marine. *No One's the Bitch: A Ten-Step Plan for the Mother and Stepmother Relationship.* (GPP Life, 2009), 6.
2. Papernow, Patricia L. *Surviving and Thriving in Stepfamily Relationships: What Works and What Doesn't.* (Routledge, 2013), 43.
3. Ganong, Lawrence H., and Marilyn Coleman. *Stepfamilies: Love, Marriage, and Parenting in the First Decade.* (Springer, 2017).
4. Graves, Robert. *The Greek Myths: The Complete Edition.* (Penguin, 2017).
5. Hand, David, dir. *Snow White and the Seven Dwarfs.* (Walt Disney Productions, 1937).
6. Geronimi, Clyde, Wilfred Jackson, and Hamilton Luske, dirs. *Disney's Cinderella.* (Walt Disney Productions, 1950).
7. Papernow, Patricia L. *Surviving and Thriving in Stepfamily Relationships: What Works and What Doesn't.* (Routledge, 2013), 8.
8. Papernow, Patricia L. *Surviving and Thriving in Stepfamily Relationships: What Works and What Doesn't.* (Routledge, 2013), 27.
9. Papernow, Patricia L. *Surviving and Thriving in Stepfamily Relationships: What Works and What Doesn't.* (Routledge, 2013), 9.
10. "Understanding the Stress Response." *Harvard Health Publishing*, accessed April 3, 2024, https://www.health.harvard.edu/staying-healthy/understanding-the-stress-response.
11. Drucker, Peter. *The Effective Executive: The Definitive Guide to Getting the Right Things Done.* (Harper Business, 2006).
12. Kennedy, Becky. *Good Inside: A Guide to Becoming the Parent You Want to Be.* (Harper Wave, 2022).
13. Aristotle. *The Nicomachean Ethics*, trans. W. D. Ross, (Oxford University Press, 1908).
14. Cascio, Christopher N., Matthew Brook O'Donnell, Francis J. Tinney, Matthew D. Lieberman, Shelley E. Taylor, Victor J. Strecher, and Emily B. Falk, "Self-affirmation activates brain systems associated with self-related processing and reward and is

reinforced by future orientation," *Social Cognitive and Affective Neuroscience* 11, no. 4 (2016): 621–629, https://doi.org/10.1093/scan/nsv136.

15. Cameron, Julia. *The Artist's Way: A Spiritual Path to Higher Creativity*. (TarcherPerigee, 2016).

16. Nagoski, Emily, and Amelia Nagoski. *Burnout: The Secret to Unlocking the Stress Cycle*. (Ballantine Books, 2020), 209.

17. McMillan, Michael. *Pink Bat: Turning Problems into Solutions*. (Simple Truths, 2009).

18. Sincero, Jen. *You Are a Badass: How to Stop Doubting Your Greatness and Start Living an Awesome Life*. (Running Press, 2013).

19. Roche, Joyce M. *The Empress Has No Clothes: Conquering Self-Doubt to Embrace Success*. (Berrett-Koehler Publishers, Inc., 2013).

20. DeLongis, Anita, and Amy Zwicker, (2017). "Marital Satisfaction and Divorce in Couples in Stepfamilies," *Current Opinion in Psychology* 13: 158–161, https://doi.org/10.1016/j.copsyc.2016.11.003.

21. Jung, Carl. *Memories, Dreams, Reflections*. (Vintage, 1989).

22. Knight, Sarah. *F*ck No!: How to Stop Saying Yes When You Can't, You Shouldn't, or You Just Don't Want To*. (Voracious/Little, Brown and Company, 2019).

23. Knight, Sarah. *F*ck No!: How to Stop Saying Yes When You Can't, You Shouldn't, or You Just Don't Want To*. (Voracious/Little, Brown and Company, 2019), 44.

24. Knight, Sarah. *F*ck No!: How to Stop Saying Yes When You Can't, You Shouldn't, or You Just Don't Want To*. (Voracious/Little, Brown and Company, 2019), 48.

25. Knight, Sarah. *F*ck No!: How to Stop Saying Yes When You Can't, You Shouldn't, or You Just Don't Want To*. (Voracious/Little, Brown and Company, 2019), 48–49.

26. Seuss, Dr. *Happy Birthday to You!* (Random House, 1959).

27. Perel, Esther. *Mating in Captivity: Unlocking Erotic Intelligence*. (HarperCollins, 2006).

28. Scott, Sharon. *Peer Pressure Reversal: An Adult Guide to Developing a Responsible Child*. Second ed. (HRD Press, 1997).

29. Papernow, Patricia L. *Surviving and Thriving in Stepfamily Relationships: What Works and What Doesn't*. (Routledge, 2013), 79.

30. Papernow, Patricia L. *Surviving and Thriving in Stepfamily Relationships: What Works and What Doesn't*. (Routledge, 2013), 45.

31. Bjornsen, Sally. *The Single Girl's Guide to Marrying a Man, His Kids, and His Ex-Wife: Becoming a Stepmother with Humor and Grace.* (New American Library, 2014).

32. Buddha. *The Dhammapada: The Sayings of the Buddha*, trans. Eknath Easwaran, (Nilgiri Press, 2007).

33. "Overcoming Resentment as a Stepmom with Beth McDonough." *Stepmomming Made Easy*, performance by Beth McDonough, Season 2, Episode 37, 5 December 5, 2023. Accessed January 21, 2025, https://stepmomming.com/ep-37-overcoming-resentment-as-a-stepmom-with-beth-mcdonough/.

34. Chanel, Coco. *The Gospel According to Coco Chanel: Life Lessons from the World's Most Elegant Woman.* (HarperCollins, 2009).

35. Nagoski, Emily, and Amelia Nagoski. *Burnout: The Secret to Unlocking the Stress Cycle.* (Ballantine Books, 2020), 134.

36. Nagoski, Emily, and Amelia Nagoski. *Burnout: The Secret to Unlocking the Stress Cycle.* (Ballantine Books, 2020), 4.

37. Nagoski, Emily, and Amelia Nagoski. *Burnout: The Secret to Unlocking the Stress Cycle.* (Ballantine Books, 2020), 6.

38. Norelli, Samantha K., Ashley Long, and Jeffrey M. Krepps. "Relaxation Techniques." *StatPearls*, U.S. National Library of Medicine, accessed August 28, 2023, www.ncbi.nlm.nih.gov/books/NBK513238/.

39. Nagoski, Emily, and Amelia Nagoski. *Burnout: The Secret to Unlocking the Stress Cycle.* (Ballantine Books, 2020), 16.

40. Nagoski, Emily, and Amelia Nagoski. *Burnout: The Secret to Unlocking the Stress Cycle.* (Ballantine Books, 2020), 21.

41. "The 5×5 Rule of Life." *Cityscape Counseling*, accessed February 1, 2025, www.cityscapecounseling.com/post/5x5-rule/.

42. Hyder, Sanaa. "How to Be Kind When You're Upset with Your Partner." *The Gottman Institute*, accessed June 16, 2025, www.gottman.com/blog/how-to-be-kind-when-youre-upset-with-your-partner/.

43. Gottman, John M., and Nan Silver. *The Seven Principles for Making Marriage Work: A Practical Guide from the Country's Foremost Relationship Expert*, Second ed., (Harmony Books, 2015), 32.

44. Lisitsa, Ellie. "The Four Horsemen: Contempt." *The Gottman Institute*, accessed May 13, 2013, https://www.gottman.com/blog/the-four-horsemen-contempt/.

45. Chapman, Gary. *The 5 Love Languages: The Secret to Love that Lasts.* (Northfield Publishing, 1992.)

46. "How Cell Phones Impact Our Relationships." *Banca Mediolanum National Convention*, YouTube, September 20, 2023, accessed January 22, 2025.

47. Carlson, Richard. *Don't Sweat the Small Stuff … and It's All Small Stuff: Simple Ways to Keep the Little Things from Taking Over Your Life*. (Hyperion, 1997).

48. Shaw, George Bernard. *Leadership in the Performing Arts*. (Routledge, 2016).

49. Riter, Ted. "Conflict Isn't the Opposite of Love; It's an Opportunity for Deeper Understanding," Instagram, March 3, 2022, https://www.instagram.com/tedritertalks/reel/DFYww4RpNF5/.

50. Fremont-Smith, Ken. "Compromise: It's Not What You Think!" *The Gottman Institute*, April 5, 2021, www.gottman.com/blog/compromise-its-not-what-you-think/.

51. Matthews, Mark. *The Power of Apology: A Guide to Healing and Rebuilding Relationships*. (Balboa Press, 2013).

52. Chapman, Gary, and Jennifer Thomas. *When Sorry Isn't Enough: Making Things Right with Those You Love*. (Northfield Publishing, 2013).

53. Angelou, Maya. *Wouldn't Take Nothing for My Journey Now*. (Random House, 1993).

54. Hazlehurst, Kait. "Hey Stepmom, It's Okay to Take Up Space." Stepmomming.com, March 12, 2019, stepmomming.com/okay-to-take-up-space-struggling-stepmom/.

55. Brown, Brené. *Daring to Set Boundaries: The Courage to Love Ourselves*. Oprah.com, https://www.oprah.com/spirit/how-to-set-boundaries-brene-browns-advice.

56. Beattie, Melody. *Codependent No More: How to Stop Controlling Others and Start Caring for Yourself*. Spiegel & Grau, 2022.

57. Robbins, Tony. Facebook, 11 July 2017, www.facebook.com/TonyRobbins/posts/if-you-talk-about-it-its-a-dream-if-you-envision-it-its-possible-but-if-you-sche/10155611946079060/.

58. Covey, Stephen R. *The 7 Habits of Highly Effective People: Powerful Lessons in Personal Change*. (Free Press, 1989).

59. Manson, Mark. *The Subtle Art of Not Giving a F*ck: A Counterintuitive Approach to Living a Good Life*. (HarperOne, HarperCollins, 2016).

60. Lewis, C.S. *The Four Loves*. (Harcourt, 1960).

Index

Note: Page numbers in **bold** refer to tables and figures.

Printed and bound by CPI Group (UK) Ltd, Croydon, CR0 4YY

27/08/2025

14725039-0001